Fleeing the Fates of the Little Rascals

By

Laura June Kenny

authorHOUSE

1663 LIBERTY DRIVE, SUITE 200
BLOOMINGTON, INDIANA 47403
(800) 839-8640
www.authorhouse.com

First published by AuthorHouse 07/22/04

ISBN: 1-4184-3863-4 (e)
ISBN: 1-4184-3862-6 (sc)
ISBN: 1-4184-3861-8 (dj)

Library of Congress Control Number: 2004093814

Printed in the United States of America
Bloomington, Indiana

This book is printed on acid-free paper.

Laura June Williams, Fall 1932

ACKNOWLEDGEMENTS

To write about a span of thirty years, the three decades that comprised the middle of the twentieth century, requires many hours of research. I was assisted and supported in this research, and in the writing of this book, by many persons, whom I wish now to acknowledge.

My thanks go to Valerie Yaros, Historian of the Screen Actors' Guild, for her encouraging support and for identifying some faces in the Cohn-Berlin photograph. I am indebted to my brother Roger for some information. Thanks, too, to Pat Calhoun, Jack's widow, who filled in a lot of blanks, with recollections of times and places. To all those friends who saved and gave me clippings about the *Little Rascals*, through the years, I say "thanks." Susan Bolt kept me on my toes each week with her letters of encouragement. My friend and dentist, Dr. Richard Swatt, supplied the back-cover photo.

For getting me back on track, writing, I am indebted to Steve Lukits, of Ontario, Canada, one-time editor of the *Kingston Whig-Standard*. Thanks go to Lynn Franklin, who always had faith this book could be written. Dan Heise, of 1st Books, was in my corner, cheering me on, from the inception of this book. To my friends, Irma Franklin and Cora Curtis, who waited patiently for fourteen months, while I lay aside the editing of their memoirs to begin my manuscript, I say, "Thanks, ladies." My friend Roslyn Kreeger, who saved articles for me and supplied further data, as needed, was never more than a phone call or an e-mail distant from my quest for information.

She consented to read the manuscript, for which I am very grateful. Finally, I want to thank our son Nathan, who came to my rescue many a day by directing me to invaluable internet sources, and he served constantly to boost my spirits!

For my children and my grandchildren,
And for all the children I have ever taught,
Written with thanksgiving
To those patient therapists
Who helped me find the steps
To the dance of Life,
And finally got me off on the right foot.....
The late Clare Hoover, M.A., and
Dr. Jeanine Berry, M.D.

With special thanks I acknowledge
The love and support
Of my husband Clifford,
And of my friend and mentor,
Elisabeth Kubler-Ross, M.D.

*"Should you shield the canyons from the windstorms,
you would never see the beauty of their carvings."*

Elisabeth Kubler-Ross, M.D.
(Used with permission.)

*"We are shaped by those who love us,
and those who refuse to love."*

Rev. John Powell, S.J.
(Used with permission.)

CONTENTS

PREFACE

The houselights in the movie-theater darken, music from the soundtrack fills the darkness, the title of the film and the cast credits are flashed momentarily, and the scene and mood are set. Then there appear those characters, who seem, oh, so much larger than life. Sometimes a single face, or a pair of heads, fills the entire screen. Is it any wonder that our society regards those visual images, and the people who project them, as super-sized human beings, celebrities worthy of undue awe and a kind of worship? There is even a new book, just published, called *Fatal Distraction*, which attempts to examine the widespread addiction that its author, Emmi Fredericks, terms *celebreholism*.

Truly the **medium** of movies, for now over eighty years, has often sent the **message** of a certain grandiosity, that somehow, real life is not large enough, that a normal childhood might be dull and monotonous. In this era of twenty-four hour cable news on television, the fate of being a celebrity is made to look and to sound as if it would be the epitome of excitement and fulfillment. Rarely are the pitfalls of the attainment of celebrity put beneath the microscope of public scrutiny.

Over seventy years ago, and for a period of three years, I sat on a welcoming lap, night after night, in a great old movie-house on Crenshaw Boulevard in Los Angeles. Embraced in the loving arms of a mother-like figure, I watched most of the movie stars, prominent from 1932 to 1935, make their appearance before my eyes, until the toddler I was, fell asleep.

Going to the movies meant, to me, being held and cuddled, till the sandman shut my eyes.

During those same three years, and for a few years after, I would, on occasion, visit movie-sets and appear momentarily as an "extra" in Hal Roach's *Our Gang Comedies*, featuring his *Little Rascals*. These film "shorts" were featured between the two main films a theater would highlight on its marquee. During the dreary economic Depression of the early 1930s, these comedy shorts produced much needed laughter, focusing as they did on the antics of ordinary children.

But the making of commercial films is not an ordinary event in the life of any child or group of children. Behind the scenes depicted, I was to discover that movie production is hard work for all concerned, and consumed, what seemed to me, endless hours, at the end of which was a fatigue no child should ever have to experience. Was this undue fatigue the only so-called "Curse of the Little Rascals," so touted by the tabloid forms of media? No, indeed, as you will learn in the unfolding of my life-story.

Why was I able to escape the ill fates and untimely ends of many former Little Rascals? Therein lies the tale I am about to tell. So many images come to mind when one finally begins to record a personal history. It is as if you stand before the tapestry that depicts the events of your life, and you behold the beauty of the fabric itself: its highs and lows, its shimmering and dull parts, and how all this hangs together and blends so well. As any weaver knows, seated before a loom, there are the permanent, set strands of thread, fastened to the framework of the loom, that make the art of weaving possible. They are called the *warp* of the fabric. The weaver then passes in and out with a spindle of thread, called the *woof*, and thus the making of whole cloth begins. It's the same for a whole life.

If I could name the *warp* that forms the basis of my life, I would have to call it what Ralph Waldo Emerson terms the mightiest aspect of "The universe alive.....the law of Compensation." He elaborates on that law: "Justice is not postponed. A perfect equity adjusts its balance in all parts of life.....The dice of God are always loaded." That dice-casting Master Weaver has somehow continually sought to balance off the profound losses and missteps of my life with the advent of grace-filled people and events, *compensation* beyond all my expectations and certainly, well beyond my human requirements. These *compensations* spared me the ill fates of many other Little Rascals!

And what to call the *woof* that was woven in and out, over and over, forming the fabric of my life? I have named it *connectedness*. Alfred Lord Tennyson says it so well for me: "I am a part of all that I have met." Early on, as a matter of sheer survival, I reached out to connect with other human beings, with animals, and with the beauty of flowers, language and music. To steady myself with all these connections, I developed a keen awareness of time and space, not in any mathematical way, but just so I could position myself at any given time. An elaborate system of *connectedness* helped me escape "The Curse."

Any human life, being described and depicted, contains a myriad of objective data or facts. The light thrown upon them, to examine them, is also of importance. For six years I lived in the desert of California, and came to know the beauty of the stark, treeless, rock-ribbed mountains surrounding my home. I studied those heights in the particular light, which each season, with the variance in the sun's rays, casts upon them. And I came to discover that it was "the light of winter" which bathed the mountains in an exquisite beauty, demarcating the peaks from the canyons, by the shadows cast upon the latter. Now in the early winter of my own life, I view it, blessing the "low-points" as well as the "mountain-top" experiences of living. I treasure the windstorms that carved my canyons! And I see so clearly that I was shaped by those who loved me, and those who refused!

Before I begin my story, I wish to acknowledge fully, and with gratitude, the contributions of my Mother to the writing of it. She managed to save, through various moves of our family, many articles, artifacts and photographs, which she passed on to me. Further, she encouraged me to begin my own collection of memorabilia. Without such saved keepsakes, this book could not have seen "the light of day." Some years before her death, Mother wrote me, "I'm hoping that you involve yourself in writing as soon as possible. I've always known that with your vivid descriptions and your perception of beauty, mental, spiritual and physical, that you will have much to offer." This book is that offering. Mother was a lover of the use of language, to say the least.

Mother was, as well, — to use the description of my mentor, Elisabeth Kubler-Ross, — in a very strange way, "The greatest teacher of unconditional love you could have had." Mother died in 1995, so my thanks for her contributions are offered posthumously.

I hope the reader will find something of interest or of meaning in the story I share. But were there no readers at all, I would still have to have told what I saw, heard, tasted, smelled, touched and felt. I would still feel impelled to comment on what I have learned along the way. I would still have to describe growing up in a Hollywood and a Southern California that is no more but must not be unsung and forgotten. Finally I would still have to exult in the exhilaration of "dancing on the earth" for my allotted time, and escaping what might well have been a pathway of darkness, even tragedy.

Laura June Kenny

CHAPTER 1

THE SMELL OF EUCALYPTUS AND THE SOUND OF MOURNING DOVES
1932-36

"Lights! Camera! Action!" That is not what I heard at the time I was given a movie "screen test" in my fifth year of life. Rather it was the soft, pleading voice of director Frank Capra, asking me to sing, to recite, and to emote. And I would not!

Though I repressed the memory of that traumatic adventure into film making for twenty-five years, I can now recall vividly just where I stood in a circle of light and heat from the stage lamps. The test took place in a huge sound stage of Columbia Pictures on Gower Street in midtown-Hollywood. I remember Mr. Capra gently exhorting me to demonstrate what I could do. I had already sung in public for a Lion's Club Christmas program a year and more before, when I was only three-and-a-half. My literary, elocution teacher Grandmother had previously taught me to memorize and recite "The quality of mercy" speech from Shakespeare's *The Merchant of Venice* at an age when I could neither read nor write yet. I was dainty, well-mannered, blue-eyed, with long, brown curls, but I didn't "want to be in pictures."

1

What I do now recollect is the powerful emotion I felt that day, and it was not "stage-fright." At that particular instant, at the center of a spotlight, I would stubbornly refuse to do what I knew I could do, and what I had been trained to do. I would "withhold" my performance because it was precisely what my birth mother wanted me to do. For those few minutes, the choice for my future was in my tiny hands, and I seized it, albeit quite unconsciously. The ball was in my court, so to speak, and I would not fling it back into play.

Most of that fifth year of my life is very faint, very vague in my memory, because it had been a year of turmoil. The Christmas I was four-and-a-half, sometime before the screen test, my baby brother, aged twenty-two months, had died of a brain tumor at Los Angeles Children's Hospital. It was then I was returned reluctantly from the care of loving foster parents who had looked after me for the better part of the three previous years.

That caring couple were "Mama Lee" and "Daddy Carl" Ingram, a middle-class and childless pair, who had read in a newspaper of the plight of my own impoverished parents, unable to care for their four children in the midst of the Great Depression. Those desperate parents of mine were seeking foster parents to feed and clothe and care for their children. It was November 1932. Franklin D. Roosevelt had just won the election for the Presidency of the United States, defeating the incumbent President Herbert Hoover.

For Mama Lee I would have done anything that fateful day at the Columbia studio, — sing, dance, recite. Before she began fulltime care of me in the fall of 1932, Lee had been a top-notch telephone operator. As well she was an accomplished musician, playing piano, banjo and saxophone. But that day of the screen test, she was not at the studio, nor for that matter, not very much in my life anymore. At some level, I knew if I made it big "in the movies," I would lose contact with Lee and Carl. They would be shut out of my life, maybe for good. And I adored them!

While I was in her care, Mama Lee had already accompanied me previously to the movie sets of Hal Roach's *Our Gang*, now known as the *Little Rascals*. These one and two-reeler "shorts" would be scheduled by movie theater managers to appear between two feature length films. (Feature length films were shorter in duration in those days.) And Saturday matinees would regularly display them among a host of short films directed to entertain children.

Mama Lee's best friends were telephone operators at major studios in Hollywood. They always let her know when there was a need for children to serve as "extras" for group or crowd scenes. Besides, she had enrolled me in dancing lessons with The Meglin Kiddies, a booking agency for young dancers and "extras." Fifty years after it was filmed, I saw a *Little Rascals* episode on television, and recognized myself by the bright plaid dress I was wearing, a dress Mama Lee had made for me. I was seen in that episode for just a fleeting moment. I was three at the time. The short was called *Mike Fright*, a film released in August 1934.

The Christmas I was three-and-a-half, I was "home" for a visit with my birth parents in Hollywood. A well-to-do Hollywood show business couple, Tillie and Max Winslow, had called the wife of the publisher of the *Hollywood Citizen-News*, to inquire if there were a family "down on their luck," a family whom the Winslows might "help out" that Christmas. The publisher's wife said her son knew some "nice boys" who came from a very poor but respectable family. Thus Tillie and Max Winslow paid a visit to our house, came into my life, and later became my second set of foster-parents.

When first introduced to Mrs. Winslow, my Grandmother would recall that I answered the question, "How old are you, Laura June?" with this quaint reply, "Half-past-three." That response charmed Tillie Winslow on the spot.

But I was not to deepen my relationship with the Winslows until my permanent return to live in a big house, with my birth family. The house this family rented from the bank for $25.00 a month was an abandoned old Hollywood mansion located at 1333 North Stanley Street. My return occurred when my brother Dickie died in December 1935. Mr. and Mrs. Winslow "helped out" with the funeral and cremation expenses.

The death of a child in a family always casts a long shadow. It was into that dark shadow of profound loss that I returned to live with my birth parents, my three older brothers and my maternal Grandmother. At four-and-a-half, I could not fill the void that was left by the death of that beautiful little auburn-haired boy. Depression, anger and unrelenting sorrow and poverty marked the atmosphere of that familial home. For my own part, I was not grieving Dickie's death, as I hardly knew him. Rather I mourned the sudden rupture of my relationship with Mama Lee and Daddy Carl!

It was a warm and pleasant household trio that, for the three previous years, had lived at 1709 W. Gage Ave., the Ingram bungalow, — Mama Lee, Daddy Carl and me, plus a shepherd-mix dog, named Teddy. I was literally enveloped with love from that dear couple. One of my first memories is of climbing out of my crib and going to their bed and lying, snug and warm, between them. Living with Lee and Carl, I had abundant parental love, a pleasant home, dolls and toys, and warm and plentiful meals.

Roslyn and me, astride the dog, Teddy.

I even had a neighbor toddler to play with. Roslyn and I became playmates before we can remember meeting each other. To this day she is my dearest and oldest of friends. We had both gone to Meglin Kiddies Dancing School before I left the Ingrams' home. Roslyn remembers she was interviewed for a tiny part in M-G-M.'s *A Midsummer Night's Dream*, but was too small for the part. Her father worked for that studio at the time. During the Great Depression, like many Los Angeles men who had a skill, Murray had found employment in the vast complex of the trades needed for a major studio.

Though I learned the very basic shuffle-ball-change, "Waltz clog" step, at tap-dancing school, at age three and four, I surely did not shine at dancing. But no matter, the Meglin Kiddies took me along with them for their appearances in the *Our Gang* two-reelers, *Beginner's Luck*, and *The Our Gang Follies of 1936*. *Beginner's Luck* is a spoof on "stage mothers" and amateur shows in general. It was released in early 1935. Later that year, in November, I would appear as one of the one hundred youngsters in this first of Roach's two-reeler "musicals," the *Our Gang Follies of 1936*. Meglin Kiddies were again used over the three weeks of shooting schedule, an extra-long timetable for the making of one of Roach's films. These productions are notable because Carl "Alfalfa" Switzer made his first appearance in the *Beginner* short, and Darla Hood would be cast for her movie debut in the *Follies* mini-musical. Movie critics of the time were favorably impressed, and urged Depression-weary movie patrons to go and see, "An ambitious undertaking, providing eighteen minutes of solid entertainment." (*Daily Variety*) A rather good review for little kids!

Mama Lee sewed for me and taught me to sing to her piano accompaniments. Her shiny black baby grand fascinated me. She and I would go to movies while nightly Daddy Carl studied for his Masonic degree in the building adjacent to the Crenshaw Theater. One of my fondest memories is sitting on her lap watching films. She would gently scratch my back and tug on my earlobe until I fell asleep. She let me cook and garden with her, and took me everywhere. She taught me to sit quietly in the chairs in the bank while she did her banking chores. For his part, because he was a natural-born engineer, Daddy Carl handcrafted my first tricycle in his garage workshop. Carl had a huge Texas family that had relocated to California. There were frequent trips by car to visit his many transplanted relatives. I was readily accepted as part of this extended Ingram clan, and thereby had many "aunts," "uncles," a set of "Grandparents" and "cousins" galore.

In contrast, my birth parents had moved from Washington State to California in July 1932. I was thirteen months old. All but a few of their many relatives remained in the Northwest, primarily Idaho and Oregon. Times were tough, so I never knew my natural aunts and uncles and my many cousins until I was grown. Only once in a decade did my Dad's nephew and my Mother's brother come visiting with their families. The only nearby relatives were character actors Guy Kibbee and his brother Milt, and their families. The Kibbees were Mother's step-cousins. They shared the same grandfather, but that gentleman, a widower doctor, had established separate and consecutive families by two wives. The first family he fathered prior to the Civil War, and the other, during and after that conflict.

My Dad had lost both a trucking business and a home in Wapato, Washington, in the economic crash of 1929. It was the house where I was born to Hazel and Russell Williams, June 8, 1931. My birth certificate names Russell as a "pool hall manager," and Hazel as a "house-wife." My late Cousin Jessie Kibbee Sichau once told me that my Mother had brought one of my brothers to Portland, Oregon, to do "radio work" when he was about six or seven.

Since Hollywood was not only known for moviemaking but also served as a big radio broadcasting center in the early 1930's, the Williams family decided to head south to Southern California. With no work and no home, and with the faint possibility of radio work for my brother in Hollywood, the family left Washington in a 1928 Chevrolet, pulling a small trailer. They left behind, stored with friends, most of their furniture. At some level, they must have decided that if, they were going to starve, at least it would be in a climate that was warm. The trek was made early summer 1932, and my brother Paul would recall that the 1932 Olympic Games were about to begin in Los Angeles in a sports complex near the campus of the University of Southern California. The Olympic stadium was to be called the Coliseum.

But work for Dad was no more plentiful in sunny California. Food ran out, hence Mother gave the story of the family's pitiful plight to the newspapers. As a result, I went to live with the Ingrams, and my brothers went to various families. Only my foster placement worked out really well, although brother Paul found his lifelong beloved Aunt Teddy and Uncle Walter somewhere along the way.

Once, when an adult, I asked Mama Lee if my birth parents came to see me in the Ingram home very soon after I went to live with them. "No," she replied, "It was March before they drove down to see our home and visit with you." I thought that strange they had waited so long. I realize now that before my parents could gather the courage to come and see how I was faring in my foster-placement, my father and mother probably had to hear President Roosevelt declare those comforting and immortal words in his March Inaugural Address: "The only thing we have to fear is fear itself." All through the years afterwards, those words had a special meaning for my Dad. He would repeat them with tears in his eyes.

I have clear memories of my playmates and neighbors on Gage Avenue, and of the Ingram house and neighborhood. To this day, I could draw an exact floor plan of that house. It was a two-bedroom bungalow, and as so often happened in those days, the Ingrams rented out the extra bedroom to an artist who worked for one of the movie studios. His name was Bush Baldridge. My photo albums show snapshots of Roslyn and me, and of the wonderful birthday parties when I was two, three and four.

While with the Ingrams, my world widened to incorporate the sounds of radio, so important in the early 1930s. There was a children's program called *Uncle Whoa Bill* that I particularly fancied, but I also enjoyed *Amos and Andy* while sitting on the lap of either Mama Lee or Daddy Carl. As well as hearing about them on the radio, I recall seeing the newspaper rotogravure photos of two big events that occurred in 1935: the birth of the Dionne Quintuplets, born in May, and the death of Will Rogers and Wiley Post in an Alaskan airplane crash in August of that year.

Then, I remember sitting one day in the Ingram breakfast nook, when Mama Lee received a phone call from my Mother. Lee begged and pleaded with my Mother that I should stay on in their home and not return to live in Hollywood. Then she cried, and later became angry that I would have to leave their home after three years. The Ingrams had offered to adopt me. My parents said, "No." So traumatic was the return to the Williams' residence that I pushed deep inside any memory of that transition. Even after years of later therapy, I could never bring to mind that repressed and painful memory, but snapshots taken soon after the return reveal a rather sad, sober and forlorn little girl.

Sad and forlorn in April, 1936.

One of a few bright spots I can call to mind, after rejoining the Williamses on Stanley Street, was a long car ride with Grandmother Reese. Other people, her friends or acquaintances, drove us to a distant garden party. I adored Grandmother, for she would read to me hour after hour, took me for long neighborhood walks and talked to me about everything, especially flowers and nature. She let me watch her do her morning exercises with wooden dumb-bells. Grandmother had become a schoolteacher in rural North Carolina when she was just age fifteen, then went on to study elocution and rhetoric in the heady Boston of the 1880's. For a brief time, Grandmother was one of that league of early feminists known as "The Bloomer Girls."

Then, a few years after, Grandmother became the first woman professor of a college in the South, the Abingdon, Virginia, "Female Seminary." There she met her future husband, and married Professor Thomas Reese, who taught classical studies. My Mother was the third of four children born to this erudite but almost always penniless couple. In a time when there was no Social Security, older, unemployed grandparents typically lived with one of their adult children. Often, long-married couples were split up to accommodate this arrangement. Thus, my Aunt Julia cared for my Grandfather Reese until his death in 1930. Previously, my Mother had taken in Grandmother to become part of the Williams household. (Leo McCarey's film, *Make Way for Tomorrow*, poignantly depicts this sad situation, which so many Depression households had to face.)

The other warm memory of that fifth year was becoming the Winslows' "little girl." Like the Ingrams, they were childless, each couple having suffered the loss of a baby, the Ingrams by a miscarriage, and the Winslows by a stillbirth. The Ingrams were a young couple in their early thirties, married for just three years, but the Winslows were older and had already been married for twenty-five years. On one of my first visits to their apartment, it was decided I should call Tillie, "Mommie Winslow," and Max became "Daddy Max."

Tillie and Max Winslow lived at the elegant Chateau Elysee Hotel at 5930 Franklin Avenue in Hollywood. The Scientology organization now occupies that stately French-style building, which has since gained landmark status. The Winslows had come to California from New York City four years after the show business newspaper *Variety* announced, "WALL STREET LAYS AN EGG," the morning after the October 29, 1929, crash of the stock market. Vaudeville had faded fast and many Broadway lights were dimmed after 1929. Radio and movies became the "in thing," and much of their production was headquartered in Hollywood.

Since Max Winslow had been in the music business for over thirty years, filmmaking and radio broadcasting might now become the new venues for his talents. Max's chief talent had always been identifying and promoting performers and songs that would become "smash hits" with the public. Around 1907 he had come upon nineteen-year-old Israel Baline, a singing waiter at a Chinatown bistro alternately called the Pelham, or more often, "Nigger Mike's." Baline parodied, with risqué lyrics, a song Winslow had promoted for the Von Tilzer song publishing firm, called "Are Ye Comin' Out Tonight, Mary Ann?" Winslow was not so shocked with the saucy, naughty lyrics but more impressed with the young man's innate talent. He told him so, and said, "Clean up the lyrics of your songs, make them fit for families, and I'll see to it that your songs get published." Mommie Winslow would recount this event time and again as I grew up.

The young Baline changed his name to Irving Berlin, sanitized his lyrics and polished his compositions, and Winslow was true to his word. The two became friends, and then roommates for a brief while before, and again, after Daddy Max, then thirty-four, married eighteen-year-old Tillie Barbary. Tillie was exactly nine months younger than Irving. Berlin was taken into the song publishing business with Max's mentoring, and together, the two of them would make the rounds of New York nightspots that featured music.

For nearly forty years, in our living room, we have hung two mementoes of Max's and Irving's gallivanting and promoting songs, until the wee hours of the morning. Tillie Winslow rarely accompanied the two men, but chose instead to take painting lessons and spend the long evenings with her art projects. One of these projects was to paint scenes on either side of a three-part screen. The hinged screen's frame was wooden, of course, but its panels were covered in heavy burlap. Night after night she painted, the burlap absorbing the oil paint as quickly as she could apply it. It seemed the pastoral scene on the one side, and the huge bouquet of flowers, on the other side, would never be finished. When the song-plugging duo would return at three a.m., Tillie would still be at her painting. Mommie Winslow told me Irving would tease her every night and say, "Tillie, when are you

Max Winslow, about the time he met Israel Baline.

going to finish those paintings?" Those two pieces of burlap, saturated with oil paint now hang, framed and mounted on masonite, to grace my vision every day!

In 1911, Berlin produced a ragtime piece that the young composer personally didn't like. Nor did he want Max to "plug" the song. Song promoters were called song-pluggers then. Unbeknownst to Berlin, behind his back, so to speak, Max pushed and promoted the song, for he had rightly evaluated it would become a national hit. It was, and we know it today as "Alexander's Ragtime Band."

One million copies of sheet music for "Alexander's" sold by year's end, two million by the end of 1912. Fame and fortune came Berlin's way. Thenceforth, Max would be known as the man who "discovered" Irving Berlin. Not too long after, Berlin came into Max's song publishing firm, Waterson & Snyder, as a full partner. In 1919, Berlin established Irving Berlin, Inc. and Daddy Max was made a Vice-President, partner and hands-on manager-in-chief. Together, for two decades, they were instrumental in Broadway revues, participation in *Ziegfeld Follies*, and New York City's Music Box Theater was one of their prime bases of operation.

One of the most celebrated and remarkable marriages to take place in the 1920s was that of Irving Berlin to Ellin Mackay, daughter of the head of the Postal Telegraph Company. Her grandfather had been a partner in the ownership of the silver mines of the Comstock Lode in Nevada. Catholic, socialite Clarence Mackay was utterly opposed to the marriage of his daughter to Jewish Mr. Berlin, no matter how famous and accomplished the young composer was. Ellin was sent off on a tour of Europe, her father hoping she would forget her musical suitor. The ploy did not work.

On January 4, 1926, in the morning, Daddy Max was at his office at the Berlin publishing house, and received a call from his dear friend and associate, Irving. As Max would tell it, "Irving telephoned me at nine o'clock. He asked me to come down to the apartment and bring along Tillie. We got there at eleven, and they were both there, Ellin and Irving. They sure wanted to get married right away." Mommie Winslow would often tell me through the years how the two couples then took the subway down to lower Manhattan and the New York Municipal Building. A license was obtained and the wedding ceremony took place in the office of the City Clerk, with Tillie and Max serving as witnesses, "standing up with" the couple.

"Imagine, Laura June, it was Ellin's first ride on the subway," Mommie Winslow would add, in the retelling of this romantic story.

Months later, when the Berlins returned from their European honeymoon, and Ellin was pregnant, they sought and found refuge with the Winslows at their summer home in up-state New York. Even in those days, celebrities like the Berlins were hounded and besieged by members of the press. Nobody had named them yet as "The Media" or "The Paparazzi," but the Fifth Estate was as relentless then, as it appears to us now, in going after a story, especially a love story with lots of twists and turns, and family conflict!

Max had promoted the career of opera star Grace Moore when she first appeared in musical revues at the Music Box Theater. Later he would install her at Columbia Pictures to star in the first musical movie to feature classical opera music, the Academy Award Nominated *One Night Of Love*. Max was warm, affable and loved by all who knew him. And he knew anyone who was anybody in show business!

Max was Jewish, raised in Boston, of immigrant parents. Tillie was Catholic, also of immigrant parents and reared in rural Norwich, New York. Mommie Winslow never told me how the two met, but she said they "kept company" for some time before they were married in New York City on January 26, 1908. Irving Berlin, still Izzy Baline at the time, prevailed upon his Lower East Side neighborhood friend, a local official named Alfred E. Smith, to marry Max and Tillie. Smith would later become Governor of New York and a candidate for President of the United States in 1928. The birth of a seven-month stillborn baby boy took place in the early years of their marriage. Composer Berlin's eldest daughter, Mary Ellin Barrett, in her book about her famous father, *Irving Berlin—A Daughter's Memoir*, characterized Mommie Winslow as having a personality of "ebullience," that hid from view her sadness over being childless.

Somehow my appearance in the Winslows' middle-aged life brought supreme happiness, not only to them, but also to me. Before I began kindergarten, and thus had to be home for school the next day, Mother and Dad allowed me to spend a few magical nights "sleeping over" in the Winslows' gorgeous luxury apartment. It was then, I think, Daddy Max thought he might have another "star" on his hands. Me! When Daddy Max heard me sing, and recite the poems and speeches my Grandmother had coached me to repeat, he perhaps envisioned me as another Shirley Temple. She was all the rage at the time. Thus it was Max, who called upon his good friend Frank Capra, and his boss and brother-in-law, Harry Cohn, studio-head of Columbia Pictures, to look at the possibility of a screen test for this "little girl" of his who had happened upon the scene.

In later years, when I was many times in the Capra home, Mr. Capra never let on that I had failed the screen test. But Harry Cohn, movie mogul and penny-pincher, probably never forgot, to the penny, how much the failed screen test had cost the studio. In future years, I always regarded him as scary "Uncle Harry," a man whose wrath was legend in Hollywood. If I went to his elaborate office at Columbia, in the company of Daddy Max, who would be discussing some detail of production with his irascible brother-in-law, I was reminded beforehand to be as quiet as a mouse, and "sit like a little lady." As was customary in that day and age, a child's elders were addressed with a certain decorum, using Mr. or Mrs. in formal circumstances. However, it was acceptable to call adult contemporaries of parents by the terms "Aunt" and "Uncle." Thus all the relatives, friends and some associates of the Winslows became honorary aunts and uncles in my life.

I do not remember Daddy Max questioning or even noting my non-compliance during the screen test. My reticence, to do what I had been asked to do, must have served as an indicator that I was not, nor could I ever become, "star material." But Mommie Winslow did question me. She sat at her blue taffeta dressing table, a wondering look on her face and with tears in her eyes. "Why, Laura June, couldn't you do what 'Uncle Frank' asked you to do? Tell me, dear!" I now realize the tears resulted because I had disappointed her, and probably greatly embarrassed Daddy Max, so used to identifying and promoting genuine theatrical talent.

I can't remember my reply, but I know how I felt, and whatever I said seemed to satisfy her. I didn't want anything to change in my relationship with either set of foster-parents. I wanted to maintain those two "other homes" to which I could retreat or escape from the bleakness of the house on Stanley Street. And Mommie Winslow and I never discussed that event again!

Besides, I had already spent days on movie sets when I had first appeared in scenes from the *Our Gang Comedies*. It was no picnic for a three, four or five-year-old! Only the "star performers," — "Alfalfa," Darla, "Spanky," "Porky," and "Buckwheat" – had chairs to sit on between "takes" during a ten-hour day. Not "extras" like me! If a scene itself included no place to sit, then the extras were consigned to sit on the floor of the scene, in between takes, while cameras and lighting and sound equipment were rearranged. Or maybe the director wanted to discuss something with one of the star performers, and the extras had to "hold" their positions. For my part, all I wanted was to go sit in Mama Lee's lap and take my usual afternoon nap.

One time a scene featured a gravel surface where I had sat for a "close-up." When the director said, "Cut," Darla and "Alfalfa" went to little canvas chairs to rest for a bit, but I, with two other extras, was told to stay, cross-legged, sitting on that hard gravel. It was not soft sand! At the end of that long shooting session, my little behind and thighs were deeply indented with the imprint of gravel. If that was what "being in the movies" was all about, I didn't want any part of it. To a three, four or five-year-old, there is no glamour in physical pain and hardship!

Was Mama Lee making the long drive with me from south-central Los Angeles up to Culver City as a means of earning more money for the Ingrams? No, they were in good shape financially, for Daddy Carl, with his many engineering skills, never lacked for employment even one day during the Depression. Rather, she loved the new and novel aspect of being inside those "dream factories" called the movie studios. For her, those days of filming were something of a lark. She knew I was cute and winsome, but lacked the pizzazz to make it big "in the movies!"

Totally repressed, pushed-down into my sub-conscious, is the memory of my own Mother's immediate reaction to the disastrous screen test. It must have been very traumatic. For from that time on, my principal emotion, where my Mother was concerned, was fear. She did, on occasion, look at me with a grimness and a fury that sent terror into my little body. Of course, and quite naturally, she and the family, to some extent, were disappointed with my failure to perform that day at Columbia. Had I shone as a budding little movie star, I could have been "a way out" of the privation of the Depression for my family, in a sense, a ready-made "meal-ticket" for the future.

I never knew how Dad regarded the failed screen test, for he never, ever discussed the event with me. In those years, after he lost his business to the 1929 crash, and as well by a betrayal of trust, he was a broken man, his outlook one of despair and discouragement. Not finding work easily, once he came to California, was disheartening also. Then add to all of that, Dickie's tragic death, the grief from which he never completely recovered. But I do remember his reading aloud to me, as I sat on his lap, after I returned home from my sojourn with Lee and Carl. I made my first attempts to read, sitting on his lap, while he scanned the daily newspaper. Hitler was in full control of his regime in Germany and in all the headlines, and I decoded a funny looking word that appeared to have an upright "n" and a sideways "n." That first word I learned to read was "Nazi."

Dad made bath-time special and memorable. Children of that era were often given a warm bath, followed by a cold rinse, "to close the pores," it was urged. I hated the coldwater rinse, but Dad made it bearable by concocting some fantastic adventure, exclaiming, "Listen, when you and I were up in Alaska, — the frozen north, —you never complained one bit when I dipped you in the icy water." At this repeated remark, I would both laugh and squeal. Then he would wrap me in a towel and dry me off, put on my pajamas, and tuck me in bed.

How to explain the relationship between my parents has always been a puzzle to me. My mother was a very literate and striking brunette beauty, and my Dad very handsome as well. Perhaps their physical union was the glue that held them together. I will never know how my quiet, unassuming Dad found the emotional resources to cope with the frequent, almost habitual hostility my Mother exhibited toward so many people and events. But he did, through most of the sixty-four years their marriage endured!

It was not uncommon, in the Depression, for whole families to head for Hollywood, hoping somehow to get a "break" into the movie business. Only seven years ago, I met an elderly man in Baker, California, whose family had brought him as a very young boy to the Golden State, and he too was in some of the early *Our Gang* movies.. As he grew older, and as so frequently happened, became less photogenic, his family abandoned him and returned to the eastern United States. Left in the care of strangers, and a minor, he came into the Los Angeles court system and a compassionate judge adopted and raised him.

Another little girl, Gloria, who was in some *Our Gang* episodes with me, came to Hollywood with her mother and sister, looking for fame and

Dad, who made bath-time so memorable.

fortune, let alone the next meal. That threesome lived a block or two away from the Stanley Street residence. I remember the mother asked my parents for food and financial help, and when the latter could not assist the family of three, Lee and Carl were approached. Carl never lacked for work during the Depression, so he gave them the monumental sum of five or ten dollars to tide them over.

Before I started school, I remember special days with Daddy Max at Columbia Studio. I would accompany him to visit sets of movies in production. I particularly remember the *Lost Horizon* set with its high, brilliant white Lamasery of Shangri-La. Uncle Frank Capra was directing this first of Columbia's artistic "classy" films. Hand-in-hand with Daddy Max, I stood in awe before what studio artists had created. In these present days, when most pictures are shot "on location," using existing buildings and landscapes, it is hard to realize how a cadre of carpenters and artists, with paintbrushes and papier-mache, could create the movie sets of the 1930s, all within the confines of the huge sound stages. But they did!

I remember too Daddy Max's good friends at the studio, and visits to their offices, often up a flight of wooden steps to the second story of unpretentious barracks-like buildings. That's where the writers worked, writers like Jo Swerling and Robert Riskin. On a couple of occasions I went to the Swerling residence, out in Beverly Hills, to play with his son who was just my age. And once, I was asked to say a single line in a film on the Columbia lot: "House, —H-O-U-S-E, — house." I heard later the line was edited out, and landed on the cutting-room floor. But no matter, Daddy Max would take me to have lunch with his friends and protégés. Max, like a lot of ex-New Yorkers, had never learned to drive, and thus hired a driver or took a taxi to reach his destinations. On a sunny day, he and I were driven to the sprawling grounds of the Beverly Hills Hotel. We drew up to a cottage on the grounds, and down the steps to greet us came golden-haired, voluptuous Grace Moore, the opera diva venturing into movie making under Max's tutelage. She took one look at me, enveloped me in a hug and said, "Oh, Max, she's adorable." Then we adjourned to a "Room Service" lunch in her cottage. The love and warmth of her greeting remains today a tender and delightful memory.

Early summer of 1936, a handsome young man named Jack Calhoun, just twenty-one and with a chauffeur's license, entered the Winslows' employ. He would be their fulltime driver for the next six years, until he went into the Air Force, becoming like another big brother to me, and almost like an attentive son to the Winslows, till the end of their days. Jack was tall and blond, having the rugged features of a young Robert Redford. He wore no chauffeur's cap or gloves, but always dressed in a dark suit and tie. His large family had been as destitute as the Williamses during the worst years of the Depression, so he had left school and had worked since he was fifteen. Jack's forte was driving quickly through all the back streets, and knowing well the geography of Hollywood and Los Angeles. He, like I, would never forget the generosity and the thoughtfulness of the Winslows.

The summer I turned five, I sat for some very special photographs. Victor Schertzinger, composer, and director of Daddy Max's production,

Jack Calhoun, the tall and handsome chauffeur.

One Night of Love, at Columbia, dabbled in portrait photography. He had a large Spanish-type home in the swank Los Feliz district, east of Hollywood, an area of opulent homes like those of writer Aldous Huxley and director Cecil B. De Mille. One afternoon a driver called for me on Stanley Street and took me to a small professionally equipped photo studio at the back of the Schertzinger home. Mr. Schertzinger posed me in various photographs all afternoon, experimenting with different kinds of lighting and props. Mommie Winslow later chose two of them, one for their Hollywood apartment and one for the cottage at Alexandria Bay. And Mama Lee and Daddy Carl always had one in their living room.

I was posed by Mr. Schertzinger with my Bi-Lo doll.

My two foster-mothers gave me my first dolls, both memorable. Mama Lee gave me a small but beautiful little black baby doll, which I had on hand whenever I stayed at her home. Thus, when I met "Buckwheat" on the set of *Our Gang*, his color and appearance were no surprise to me. I had a doll that looked much like him. That same year, Mommie Winslow bought me a Bi-Lo doll with a porcelain head and a face that looked like that of a newborn baby. I loved to carry that doll, and one day, when out on a walk with my Grandmother, I dropped her on the sidewalk and broke her head. Mommie Winslow never scolded, but instead had a "doll hospital" send to Germany for one of the last such replacement heads to be imported into the United States before World War II. That precious doll lives with my granddaughters now!

In my red velvet coat and hat with Ben Bernie and his dog.

If Mama Lee did not sew my clothes, then Mommie Winslow bought them for me from the finest of Los Angeles department stores of the day, The Broadway-Hollywood, Robinson's, and the May Company, and especially Bullock's Wilshire. Next door to the latter was a shoe store where Mommie Winslow would buy me two and three pairs of shoes at a time. In those days there was a machine where they determined the fit of the shoes by X-raying your feet. Mommie Winslow also took me to her dressmaker, Madame Luba, and had made for me a dubonnet red velvet fitted coat and matching bonnet. For just five, I felt very elegant indeed when I wore that ensemble! I even had my picture taken with orchestra leader Ben Bernie wearing that attire.

There was the commonality of religion where Mommie Winslow and Grandmother Reese were concerned. Neither of my parents on Stanley Street ever attended any church that I can remember. Nor did Mama Lee and Daddy Carl at that point in their lives. But the Winslows and my Grandmother regularly attended the Christian Science church closest to their homes, and my brothers and I would go to the local Christian Science Sunday School. I really enjoyed the Sunday School, for the chief teaching I came away with was positive: that "God is love," and that I was somehow God's own child. The first bedtime prayer I learned to say began, "Father-Mother God, Loving me....". Lee and Carl always tucked me in, asking me to say that prayer. It would be two decades before I had to face and deal with some of the dualistic Christian Science dogma that pushed me away from that religion. But I never abandoned the basic premise that God loved me, and that I could count on that love being manifested in a visible way in my life.

Somewhere along the line, and in the same time frame, Mother applied for the new Social Security cards the federal government was issuing to anyone that held employment. My middle brother and I received some of the first Social Security cards issued in California. We have compared our eight-digit numbers, and we are only a few numbers apart. Probably my two other brothers received their cards early, for Mother had learned about Central Casting, where your name, age, physical description and photograph would be put on file with your address and telephone number.

When the Hollywood studios needed to film group or crowd scenes, Central Casting would locate and make the call for the number of "extras" needed. That call meant "work" and "income" for an impoverished family. If such an "extra" were a school-aged child, there would be a trip to the downtown Los Angeles Board of Education, where a doctor examined you, and clearance was given to miss school, along with a limited work permit. Then you could proceed to the designated studio on the appointed day, and always, always, very early in the morning. This would allow for the wardrobe, make-up and hairdressing staff to make you presentable for the camera and the scenes to be shot that day. Shooting usually began at nine sharp, and often didn't end until six p.m. A long, long day for children of any age!

Why did I title this chapter, "The Smell of Eucalyptus and the Sound of Mourning Doves?" The simple answer is this: that particular smell and that particular sound were the only sensory "constants" or "givens" I could cling to in those first five years of my life after the family's move to California. Whichever household I was with, in whichever home I woke up, somewhere in the background and very palpable, I could either hear the soothing cooing of ring-necked mourning doves or smell the pungent fragrance of eucalyptus trees, or experience both. Moving between three homes and three sets of parents meant I had to steady myself psychologically by very quickly establishing myself in and fixing upon a certain "time and place." Then I would hastily observe and absorb the ambience of sights, sounds and smells associated with that specific venue. Developing an acute sensory awareness was the result. The sound of nearby voices was particularly important to me, so I became very adept, very early, at identifying who was speaking within earshot, and what the tone of one's voice implied!

To this day, I carry in my head a map of the whole Los Angeles area, Hollywood and the San Fernando and San Gabriel Valleys. I memorized the routes taken to and from each household and all the landmarks along each route. Early on, I learned the days of the week, and which days I would be going to which home. Now I am grateful for the lack of rootedness, for a prevailing sense of uncertainty, and for my missing the customary childhood security of just one home, because these very deficits became the launching pads for the *compensations* of heightened memories and the development of an inner dialogue that would always tell me where I was and where I had been, at any given time. Especially when I would be "home" with the Williams family, I would put myself to sleep remembering and reviewing the minute details of the most recent visit with either set of my foster-parents. And I would count the days, even the hours, until the next visit with either Mama Lee and Daddy Carl, or Mommie Winslow and Daddy Max!

CHAPTER 2

LIFE BECOMES A TRIANGLE IN SPACE AND TIME
1936-41

Life became a predictable routine in the fall of 1936 when I started Kindergarten. Most weekends Lee and Carl came to pick me up on Friday nights, returning me back to Stanley Street Sunday evenings. During the week, the Winslows' chauffeur Jack came to call for me after school at least once, and often two times a week. I would be taken from school to the Chateau, have lunch, then take a nap on Daddy Max's big bed, afterwards go shopping or visiting with Mommie Winslow. Then after sharing dinner with the Winslows, I would be driven back to my parents' home on weekday nights.

Cooking was never Mommie Winslow's forte. There were a few special dishes she liked to prepare, but I never sampled them till later. Instead Mommie Winslow ordered in "Room Service," making selections for breakfast, lunch and dinner from a printed daily menu slipped under the apartment's front door early every morning. The Chateau had a first-class chef who prepared beautiful, delicious fare that I can see and smell in memory even now. The same waiter, Bill, brought the trays of food for every meal, set the table in the small apartment dining room, and served the first helpings from metal containers with silver lids. The hot food was always hot, and the cold food always cold, brought in containers of crushed ice.

The Chateau Elysee was the premiere hotel and apartment house, along with the Hollywood Roosevelt Hotel and the Hollywood Plaza, in the central Hollywood area. One had to go to downtown Los Angeles to the Biltmore Hotel, or to Wilshire Boulevard for the Ambassador Hotel, or out to Beverly Hills to the Beverly-Wilshire Hotel or the Beverly Hills Hotel to find comparable luxury or elegance. There was no Century City with its present-day accommodations, for Twentieth-Century Fox Studios then occupied the land where Century City was later built.

The elegant Chateau Elysee hotel and apartment house.

The Chateau sat on almost a complete city block, surrounded by well-kept lawns, gardens and terraces. To the east of it, ran a small stream, bordered by high eucalyptus trees, and a path skirted the stream. Its garage was underneath a tennis court and adjacent rose garden and terrace. Built in the worst years of the Depression, the architects and the building's owner, Mrs. Thomas Ince, spared no expense and attended to the finest of details. The woodwork within was of dark oak, and the lobby and halls were furnished with classical French furniture. On the corner of Bronson Avenue and Franklin, beyond the shallow stream, sat an old yellow frame house, once occupied by writer Adela Rogers St. Johns and her family. And between the Chateau and the St. Johns residence was a tiny flower shop where Mommie Winslow purchased the flowers and plants that were always plentiful in her apartment.

I loved Kindergarten at Hollywood's Gardner Street School, and my teacher, Mrs. Brown. California had pioneered in the establishment of kindergartens that were like big cottages, separate from the main school buildings and set in their own spacious playgrounds. I recall the love and warmth of Mrs. Brown. At some level I knew that she knew the house on Stanley Street was not a happy home. Without words, Mrs. Brown acknowledged my particular situation, making my year of Kindergarten joyful, comforting and serene.

Dad walked me to and from Kindergarten, north on Stanley Street, to Sunset Boulevard, where we then turned east and walked toward Gardner Street. There were little shops and a bank along the way. My favorite store, in passing, was the Parisian Florist shop, to this day in that same location after eighty years. I loved to pause at its corner entrance and just smell the essence of flowers from within. When we reached Gardner Street, we did not cross Sunset Boulevard with the signal, but used an underground tunnel provided so people would not cross the streetcar tracks that ran diagonally from one corner to the other. I always held my nose and hurried when we went under Sunset Boulevard because the smell of urine reeked from the tunnel's walls.

In those long-ago days, Los Angeles had a great system of mass-transit called "The Red Cars." These sturdy old streetcars moved out from downtown Los Angeles on tracks like spokes of a wheel to the far corners of the populated areas. This particular streetcar route moved from West Hollywood's Santa Monica Boulevard on a northeasterly diagonal path that crossed Sunset Boulevard and emerged on Hollywood Boulevard at the intersection of that famous street with La Brea Avenue. We never took that same streetcar to get to school even though its tracks and right-of-way skirted the south of our big rented property. A nickel for the ride for each of us would have stretched the family's meager budget.

As we moved toward the school buildings north of Sunset, we would pass and smell the contents of the bakery, which Dad cleaned nightly. As part of his pay he would receive unsold stale bread and cake to take home and feed our family of seven. Further along Sunset we would pass the Vista Theater, now the RockWalk center, and beyond, there was a small grocery market where the men who tended the vegetables gave Dad the wilted, leftover produce. Almost always our evening meal at Stanley Street would include a platter of fresh, uncooked and peeled turnips, carrots, and celery that Dad had prepared. The main course consisted of boiled potatoes and bacon gravy. Once an old black man appeared at the kitchen door, begging for something to eat. Mother and Grandmother took pity on him, invited him in, seated him in the kitchen, and fed him stale pastries and wilted vegetables, and a cup of coffee.

There were only three families whom my Mother and Dad could call close friends beyond the Winslows and the Ingrams — Marion Pompey's, the Lady family in the San Fernando Valley, and a butcher named Arnie, who lived with his family in Santa Monica. Marion Pompey it was who had directed the Ingrams to read the 1932 newspaper article that ushered me into their foster care. The Lady family met the Williamses in the Valley, during the latter's brief stay at a rented home on Woodman Avenue, just north of Ventura Boulevard, before the move to Stanley Street. Somehow Mr. Lady provided a connection whereby Dad would give a farmer extra leftover vegetables and baked goods from the market and bakery, to feed his livestock, in exchange for milk for us to drink. Sometimes Dad took me with him to fetch the milk supply. He would drive from Stanley Street over the narrow, wooded Laurel Canyon Boulevard pass into the Valley, which was then largely agricultural. The highlight of the trip was seeing a waterfall on the canyon route.

Besides Gloria Hurst, who lived nearby and was in the *Our Gang* movies with me, when "home in Hollywood," I played with only three other little girls, one named Duba, who lived across the street on Stanley, and Phyllis Lundine, whose family had once been our neighbors when the Williams family rented a flat behind a furniture store on Sunset Boulevard. I tried to share my interest in books with Duba, but she remained unconvinced of the value of reading, telling me, "I read a book once." Once was enough for her! But Phyllis and I would stay in contact for the next forty years. She was two years younger than I. Her mother brought her to play with me because she was so timid and shy, and somehow I could draw her out of her shell. My step-cousin, Shirley Ann, daughter of actor Guy Kibbee, came into my life sometime before my sixth birthday. Shirley was ten days younger than I, and had the gorgeous Kibbee auburn hair and peaches-and-cream skin tones.

Sometimes I would be invited to stay overnight at the two-story ranch house of the Kibbees in the sparsely inhabited east San Fernando Valley. "Uncle Guy" was a seasoned character actor, and had major roles in movies like the 1936 *Captain January* with Shirley Temple. His little ranch acreage was just minutes away from both Universal Studios and Warner Brothers', then recently ensconced in the Valley after a move from their former Sunset Boulevard location. No Los Angeles freeway system in those days meant that if you had steady work at the studio, and Guy did, then you situated your home in close driving range. Besides, he loved golfing, and the Lakeside Golf Course was close at hand in Toluca Lake. Cousin Shirley would have her birthday parties at the Golf Club with its swimming pool and large dining room. Shirley Temple was often present as an honored guest, and she deserved that status, because her behavior was always both serene and gracious for one so young.

Shirley Kibbee was the only girl I knew who had a French governess, a lady named Mimi, probably hired when their household received a baby brother, Guy Junior, in 1935. Shirley had lots of toys and liked books as much as I did, but Shirley never came to play at my house, only to my birthday parties, after I returned to live at Stanley Street. Her warm and loving mother was Esther Reed, nineteen years younger than Uncle Guy, and I always called her "Aunt Brownie."

29

Laura June Kenny

Through all my visits to the Kibbee homes during the next ten years, I never saw Uncle Guy present at the breakfast table one time. He would have dinner with us, after a day of shooting movie scenes, then retire very early for the night, and rise before daylight, to get the studio wardrobe and make-up chores behind him before filming began, at nine o'clock. His family-depriving schedule further served to underline my observation that movie making was not a recipe for family togetherness. I felt sorry for my cousins Shirley Ann and Guy Junior. Their dad was already in bed and asleep, — never around, — when it was time for them to be tucked in.

Guy's career in movies was prolific. He was part of that cadre of solid character actors and actresses that each studio called upon to flesh out their film productions. Over twenty-plus years, he appeared in one hundred twenty films, most notable of which were *Rain*(1932), *Forty-Second Street*(1933), *Babbitt*(1934), *Our Town*(1940) and six of the films depicting *Scattergood Baines*(1941-43). Born in Texas in 1882, at age thirteen he broke into show business on the Mississippi riverboats, then went on to the legitimate theater before arriving in Hollywood. Frank Capra would characterize Guy's many portrayals as the embodiment of a bumbling, stumbling officialdom. An example was Capra's casting of Guy in the great Jimmy Stewart film, *Mr. Smith Goes to Washington*. Uncle Guy was to play an exasperated Governor!

I did not lack for playmates or adult friends when I was with either of the two sets of foster-parents. Mama Lee saw to it that I visited with my best friend Roslyn, even though she was no longer a neighbor child. Then there was Mary Ann Roberts, Shirley Scholine, Janie Spencer, Paul Hartman and a neighbor boy named Jackie. Lee was gregarious, and had a wide circle of friends, some single and childless, but most with at least one child. Next door to her was a childless older couple, Bertha and Billy McMahon. On weekend mornings, when Lee and Carl wanted to sleep in, I was allowed to creep out of the Ingram house and go next door to the McMahons', where I had breakfast with them. Bertha was an excellent cook, and she and I would visit at length while she made pies or rolls. I would watch in wonder, for I didn't see this skill back in my Hollywood home.

For her part, with me around, Mommie Winslow now had something in common with her many friends who had children. There were Ed and Stella North, Grace and Gus Kahn, Maurice and Alice Reingold, Frank and Lu Capra, and of course, Irving and Ellin Berlin, with their three daughters. The Norths and the Kahns had older children, teen-agers or young adults, who became role models for how I was to behave in "polite society." And I looked and listened carefully!

Maurice Reingold was a jeweler with a small display office and showroom in the Equitable Building, at the corner of Hollywood and Vine. He and his wife were the older parents of an adopted daughter, Barbara, near my age. I played with her at their Larchmont district home, and at their beach house in the Malibu Colony, before they relocated in Beverly Hills. Barbara shared her books with me. One evening, the Winslows were having dinner at the Reingold's home, with me in tow. I must have made a social faux pas at the table, and I remember "Aunt Alice" cautioning Mommie Winslow, "Tillie, you mustn't let her do that in public." I felt sorry for my foster-mother that she had to be admonished this way. From then on, I didn't want to be any kind of embarrassment to the Winslows. I wanted to have "nice manners."

The two little sons of Frank Capra, — Frankie. Jr., born a month after my little brother Dickie, and Johnny, born in 1935, — were also playmates. Their beautiful mother Lu gave me an 8x10 photo of them when Johnny was about six months old, and inscribed it to me. The Capras also had a beach house in the Malibu Colony, and I loved playing on the sand with the little boys at the edge of the Pacific Ocean.

In recent years, revisionist biographers of Frank Capra have pooh-poohed the idealism that shines out from so many Capra films. In his own autobiography, *The Name Above the Title*, Frank describes a low point in his career as a rising force at Columbia Pictures. According to his account, he was reeling from the great success of the movie, *It Happened One Night*, which had captured a number of Academy Award Oscars. He thought he could never hit a "Grand Slam" like that again, and developed a malady of fevers, sweats and weight-loss. Retreating from the studio to the bedroom

31

Frank Capra, enjoying fishing with Max Winslow, in the Thousand Islands resort on the St. Lawrence River.

of his home, the only person he welcomed into his downward-spiraling miasma was my Daddy Max. Capra really feared he was dying.

One day, Daddy Max brought a man to see Frank. Max left the two alone and went to listen to the radio in a nearby room. The man was rather plain and non-descript, but he got right to the point. He challenged "Uncle Frank" to rise from his depression, with all its mental and physical symptoms, and seize the opportunity his astute directing ability gave him. Frank would write to me of "the power of the filmmaker" in a letter years later. "I could talk to all 'for two hours, and in the dark,'" he said of his epiphany, recalling Daddy Max's contribution to this event. In his autobiography, Capra does not reveal who the man was, only the life-changing and refocusing effect the visitor's words had upon his life.

This episode has been widely scoffed at, and its timetable perhaps rightly questioned, but I know it to be true, for Mommie Winslow told me about it, even the name of the visitor, two to three years after it occurred. I recall where I was standing in her bedroom, when she told me. I remember she said that he was a Christian Science practitioner or Reader in one of that denomination's churches, but he did not come that day to preach Christian Science religion to the ailing director. Instead he performed for Frank what my favorite analyst, Viktor Frankl, would describe as logotherapy or meaning therapy. "He who has a why to live can live with almost any how," encapsulates the essence of Frankl's philosophy, honed through the devastating rigors of five years in a Nazi concentration camp. The mysterious visitor gave Frank a "Why" to revive and to live! Through film, he could communicate to millions, and "for two hours, and in the dark."

Now, too, besides young Lu Capra, Mommie Winslow could share the role of parenting with her two remaining sisters, Sarah and Rose. "Aunt Sally," as I called Sarah, was much older than Tillie and Rose, and had raised the sisters after their mother died in childbirth, when Rose was born. Sarah had only one son, but he was an adult and lived in the East. I never met him, but I knew the two sisters that "Aunt Rose" Cohn was rearing in the Mediterranean-style home on Fremont Place. They were the daughters of Harry Cohn's older brother, Max, who was widowed and had fallen on hard times. Aunt Rose had joined her sister-in-law, Jeanette Cohn, in a visit to the school where the forlorn five and three-year-old girls had been placed by their father. Rose brought them to her home, and there they grew to adulthood, deeply loved by Aunt Rose, but dominated by their controlling Uncle Harry. He was not content to run Columbia pictures with an iron hand. He had to be the total "boss" at home as well! And he didn't even live there anymore, having moved out to his own apartment in the mid-thirties, so he could carry on extra-marital affairs!

Uncle Harry and Aunt Rose were in continuing conflict over her unwillingness to grant him the divorce he wanted. Her chief deficit had been her barrenness, for he wanted a child of his very own as a symbol of his manhood! He was not content to assist in the rearing of his brother's daughters. I do not remember Judith well, but the older sister, Leonore, confided in Mommie Winslow about the struggles she had in the Cohn household with her fierce uncle. I was present to hear all about this, over tea and cinnamon toast. My little girl heart ached for Leonore, for she was very beautiful and gentle, to me like a fairy-tale princess held captive in a castle where the ruler was a tyrant!

(from l.to r.), Rose Cohn, Irving Berlin, Harry Cohn, Ellin Berlin, actor Jack Holt, and probably Dorothy Revier, his co-star in Frank Capra's 1928 film, *Submarine*. Cohn allowed only a few photos of himself. Photo courtesy of Pat Calhoun.

Besides the Christmas in 1936, there were other events I clearly remember. Mother had become pregnant that September, and though later in the pregnancy she would be confined to bed-rest, she managed to accompany me to the set of *Reunion in Rhythm*. Originally scheduled by Hal Roach to be the *Our Gang Follies of 1937*, it was renamed because, in the opening scenes, former *Our Gang* cast members were highlighted at a kind of reunion. When one considers that the 221 episodes of the *Little Rascals* were made over twenty-two years, it's plain to see there were distinct yet overlapping casts that spanned those two decades. I always say that there were the first set of Rascals who spanned the silent films and moved into the "Talkies;" then there was the group, which I joined on occasion, —the most famous group, with "Alfalfa" and "Spanky;" and finally, the last of the Rascals, the group with "Froggy," and Mickey Gubitosi. We now know the latter as Robert Blake, of present-day tragic headlines.

My recollection of this film-shoot centers on being very tired and moving to and from the studio in the darkness of November dawns and early evenings. Dad would drive Mother and me to Culver City and drop us off at the studio. I would have my hair done, make-up applied, and be dressed by wardrobe. Then, come nine a.m., the long hours of filming would begin, with a short break for lunch. We couldn't afford to eat at a nearby restaurant, so it was a peanut butter and jelly sandwich, which saw us through the lunch-hour. Dad would call for us as darkness fell over Los Angeles, and we would head north to the Hollywood area. I was too tired to eat, but do remember being spoon-fed bread and warm-milk, and barely being able to hold my head up to receive the nourishment. When it was time for my evening bath, I just held up my little arms and let my parents undress me and give me a quick warm bath, without any of Dad's fanciful story-telling. Then came merciful sleep, and the whole routine began again next morning and was repeated for days after. I made eight dollars and twenty-five cents a day as an "extra," but that put a lot of food on the table of a family of seven.

I preferred instead the games and toys of Kindergarten, the music and reading of stories by Mrs. Brown. She was especially tender and gentle with me after the days of absence from school, while I had been at the studio. Although it may have been reported that there was schooling on the set of the Rascals, during the film shoots of the seven episodes I appeared in, I do not recall once when I ever saw a studio schoolteacher, on hand, and instructing anybody.

The Christmas of 1936 I will never forget! Of course, I had been to the department stores with both Mommie Winslow and Mama Lee during my weekly stays in their households. Lee and Carl got a kick out of my going to see Santa Claus and telling him what I wanted for Christmas. There was a big Sears and Roebuck store at the corner of Slauson and Vermont

DETACH FOR YOUR RECEIPT

SOCIAL SECURITY ACT
ACCT. NO._____

LAURA JUNE WILLIAMS   DATE NOV – 6 1937

GROSS EARNINGS	ST. UNEMP. INS.	FED. O.A. PEN.	OTHER DEDUCTS
8.25	.07	.08	

HAL ROACH STUDIOS, INC.

My pay slip from Hal Roach Studios, Inc.

Avenues, and I paid a visit there and sat on Santa's lap. Oh, how I wanted a Shirley Temple doll, complete with golden ringlets! Thank goodness, Santa didn't promise anything specific, but inquired, for sure, whether I had been "a good girl."

As for Mommie Winslow, Christmas was a time when she could open her generous heart for a multitude of people. Hadn't she come upon the Williams family just two Christmases previously, the first time I met her? Now I accompanied her on the many shopping expeditions to buy dozens of gifts for friends and relatives. She put a great deal of thought into what each person should receive from her and Max. They had the means, so money was no object. Even more than this, the wrapping of the gifts was, for her, a work of art. She set up two card tables in her living room at the Chateau, and they would be there for two months prior to the big day. In these pre-Hallmark days, she had all the tools at hand: various colored tissue paper, scissors, scotch tape, stickers, stars, ribbons of every color, and most of all, beautiful things that she had cut from magazines and Christmas cards sent to her the year before. I watched in awe as she worked with each gift and each gift box. The finished present was often more beautifully wrapped and more meaningful than what was inside as the gift. People didn't want to open their packages, they were so lovely! In later years, I would call Mommie Winslow "the patron saint of gift-wrapping."

When I was with Lee and Carl, they would get their Christmas tree early and I would help them decorate it. Their living room was large so we could get a tall and wide tree. The Winslows, on the other hand, had a spacious living room, but it was furnished with the many antiques Tillie loved to collect. If they bought a tree, it would have to sit atop a marble table, so Tillie would purchase a small silver-spruce. But there were other ways she brought the Christmas season alive. Always there was a large cyclamen plant with abundant blooms and one or more poinsettias. But the most beautiful Christmas decoration was hung on the outer door of apartment 116 at the Chateau. Somewhere Mommie Winslow had found a set of a dozen cascading golden bells that tinkled at the touch of a hand. She hung them, suspended from a large, bright red velvet bow with velvet ribbons. I knew I could count the days till Christmas when I saw the golden bells on that front door!

There was a Christmas program at school, and Mrs. Brown chose me to sit as a doll under the large Christmas tree on the auditorium stage. I guess she chose me because she knew I could sit very still, as I had for my part in the Rascals. I wore a tiered dress of light pink organza, and steadily stared right out at the audience with a slight smile on my face. (Decades after my performance, the Gardner Street School auditorium would be named for Michael Jackson, the most famous, or maybe infamous, of the school's alumni.)

Hard to believe, but Los Angeles, and the Hollywood section of it, had plenty of vacant lots in the 1930s, even on Sunset Boulevard. There were few apartment houses in contrast to the almost unending multitude of those existing today. Next to a four-story apartment house on the corner of Stanley and Sunset, there was the vacant lot to which my Dad and brothers went in search of a tree for our family, on Christmas Eve. Most trees had been sold. But a few big ones, tall ones, were left, and could be purchased for ten cents a foot, if the tree-seller wasn't moved by Christmas cheer to just give it away at that late hour. A big tree was surely needed, for the old mansion's living room was big enough for my brothers to toss around a football. I remember an old leather rocker and an upright piano as the only pieces of furniture the room usually held.

I came down the stairs on Christmas morning, my eyes enchanted by the sight I beheld. There was a huge tree, and it had been decorated modestly late Christmas Eve. But underneath it was a profusion of presents, with something for everybody, but most gifts were earmarked for me. I did not receive the Shirley Temple doll, but there were plenty of other playthings. One especially big baby doll I named Maxine, for Daddy Max. There were two doll beds, one a small, canopied four-poster, which Mama Lee and Daddy Carl had put together for me. And the second was from "Aunt Grace" and "Uncle Gus" Kahn, lyricists and composers. It was of solid wood with sides that went up and down like a real baby's crib. Mommie Winslow gave me a set of small porcelain blue willow pattern dolly dishes. Later that week, a truck came to our house to deliver a bedroom set in the California Mission style, —a twin bed, a dresser and a bureau with a matching mirror. I felt like a little princess in my bedroom upstairs, the best of the four bedrooms, because it had a sun-drenched Victorian cupola at one corner.

Winter turned into the spring of 1937. Mother developed a heart condition in her pregnancy, which meant she could no longer climb stairs, so the bed she shared with Dad was moved down to the dining room. As the dining room was also a big room, with a mock fireplace, there was even room enough to contain our oval oak table and the chairs for the seven of us.

In pre-World War II Los Angeles, Jews were personas non-gratis in the Southland's golf clubs and clubhouses. So Los Angeles Jewry formed its own golf club –The Hillcrest. Daddy Max was a member, as were many show business folks and some industrialists. His favorite partner for cards and poker was Chico Marx, one of the trio of comedic brothers. Sometimes in the late afternoons, Jack Calhoun, the Winslows' driver, would take me with him to call for Daddy Max at the end of an afternoon of golf and cards. I would go inside the club and find Daddy Max and the piano-playing Marx brother just finishing a poker game, usually for high stakes. According to his daughter's own account of her father, written years afterwards, Chico was a compulsive gambler. He dearly loved his then teenage daughter, Maxine, thus he related to me easily, and I liked him, even without his trademark black wig and pointed hat.

Chico and his brothers, Harpo and Groucho, had just finished filming one of their funniest comedies, *A Day at the Races*, and Chico suggested Daddy Max and Mommie Winslow bring me to the scheduled premiere at Grauman's Chinese Theater. Prior to the film's first showing, the Marx Brothers went to the Brown Derby restaurant near Hollywood and Vine Streets. The Winslows and I had gone there for dinner also. The brothers and their dinner guests dispersed to separate tables throughout the big restaurant, but during the meal, one of them would occasionally stand up, look out at the other diners, and make a funny remark. At this, another of the threesome would stand up and retort in kind, and, if you were lucky enough to be a diner in the Derby that night, you had one of their stage routines unfolding over dinner. There was hysterical laughter throughout the Derby, and even a six-year-old could appreciate the hilarity!

Mommie Winslow told me later that this episode reminded her of an evening when she and Daddy Max were in Chicago, many years before, and went to a dinner party at the home of the Marx Brothers' mother, Minnie. Dinner was served at a long table with maybe sixteen people in attendance. One of the brothers would say, "Pass the rolls, please!" With this cue, another Marx Brother would rise from his chair and literally pass a roll, through the air, like a small football, to his hungry brother. And so it went for the entire meal, through every course!

I loved being part of a Hollywood premiere, the only one I ever attended. I remember the klieg lights, and the red-carpet treatment as the Winslow's black Buick pulled up to the curb in front of Grauman's, and Jack opened the door for us to walk through the famous courtyard with its myriad hand and footprints of movie stars.

There was a disastrous flood in the Ohio and Tennessee Valleys that winter. On the radio, the Red Cross put out calls for donations to meet the basic needs of the disaster's victims. Around that time, Daddy Max would sometimes go to the horse races at Santa Anita. He asked me if I would like him to bet on the up-and-coming favorite, the great Seabiscuit. Whenever the latter won, and I received the winnings, I wanted to take them and send them to the Red Cross. My Dad was very agreeable to that altruistic outcome. The Winslows were also pleased that I was putting the needs of others first, at a very young age.

Sometime that spring, the Ringling Bothers, Barnum and Bailey Circus came to town and set up shop down in the uninhabited open fields near the Pico and Robertson intersection. Yes, there were vast vacant areas of Los Angeles then, big enough for all the trailers, cages and tents of the circus. Daddy Max took me, and my brother Paul. We three spent a wonderful afternoon under the "Big Top." Elephants were used to hoist the canvas "Big Top" in place, when the circus came to town on railroad cars.

Mother's mother, Grandmother Reese, lived with us, but she was incapable of taking care of the household chores Mother could no longer do, because of her precarious pregnancy. Grandmother's years as a teacher, and her literary interests, had never prepared her for practical housekeeping chores, although she was an exemplary and wonderful baby-sitter for me, reading to me and taking me for long walks. Mama Lee came to the rescue, offering her own mother, Grandma Shaffer, to come and take care of the household. Lilly Belle Shaffer was a woman of many down-to-earth talents: cooking, sewing, and cleaning, among them. She slept in my room and got me ready for Kindergarten each morning. Then one morning, June 11, 1937, I awoke to hear the cry of a baby, and Grandma rushed into my room to say I had a baby sister who would be called Joyce Lee.

Grandma Shaffer, whom I dubbed "Gram," stayed for some weeks after Joyce's birth, until Mother was on her feet again. I returned with Gram later that summer to the mountain cabin or cottage that she maintained in Kagel Canyon, a narrow wooded area just north of the San Fernando Valley. Single-handedly, Gram had taken a shack in the mountains in the mid-1920s, and made of it a home, a little lodge with sleeping places for a crowd, if need be. The Winslows were gone, as usual, to their summer home in the Thousand Islands of upstate New York. I would not see them again until late September when they would return to Hollywood. They did not depart on the old Santa Fe Super Chief until my birthday party had taken place three days before Joyce's birth. The summer was long, and I missed them!

The Winslow summer home in upstate New York.

But picture post cards, with scenes of the Thousand Islands, came often in the mail from the Winslows. Occasionally there would be a letter, which Grandmother would read aloud to me. In late June, Mommie Winslow wrote, "Remember our promise." I don't now recall what we had promised one another, but that phrase demonstrates how bonded we had become. Daddy Max, whose handwriting was atrocious, rarely wrote to me, but this time, he added this postscript: "My love to you, my little darling."

Now, Grandma Shaffer's "cabin" became a third home to which I could escape or retreat. I was company for her and she taught me so much, and allowed me great freedom to roam her hillside. Gram had a player piano and she showed me how to insert and remove the paper rolls, how to pump the pedals and how to produce wonderful piano melodies. I sang along because the words were printed on each roll, and I could read a little. She had very few books to look at, so I was left to improvise for play. Her yard was big with various terraces as it cascaded down the hillside to a ravine. She had reinforced these terraces by stonewalls, and with concrete she had mixed herself.

Gram's cabin had many rooms at various levels, because she had added them, without a lot of professional help, from time to time. There were lots of step-downs, and her bedroom, at the top of the house, was accessed by narrow stairs. It was a small room with windows on all four sides, just big enough for her double bed, a tiger maple dresser and a single chair. We would lie there at night, under her down comforter, and listen to the wail of the coyotes on the hillsides. Then she would tell me about her days as a girl in Iowa, and as a clerk in a store, and of her marriage to Lee's father, Charlie, the train engineer who left her a widow after twenty years of marriage. She had a great and unusual memory for detail, and for days and dates that things had happened in her life. I wanted to be like her, and I thought that all grown-ups had this remarkable ability. So I deliberately began to categorize happenings in much the same fashion as she did.

The cabin had no indoor plumbing except for cold running water for the kitchen sink. There was a kerosene stove and a wood cook stove. Nighttimes we took a "slop jar" upstairs, but daytimes we had to make use of an outhouse that Gram had dubbed the "Duck Inn." It even had a sign noting that name in the shape of a duck. To take a bath, water was heated on the wood stove and you stood in an old tub and washed yourself. Or if the day had been particularly warm, you waited until late afternoon, then went into an outside wooden stall topped by a showerhead. The showering device was attached to a hose that held water, now very warm from being in the hose all day, in the sunshine. The latter form of bathing was more fun for me than just standing in a tub next to the wood stove.

Gram had no phone, so visits were pre-planned and of set length, allowing for Mama Lee and Daddy Carl to bring me to the cabin or pick me up there. I loved seeing them again when they called for me, but I hated to say good-bye to Gram, and could hardly wait for the next vacation time I could spend with her.

However, something exciting was going to take place for the balance of the summer. I needed to be back in Hollywood. Daddy Max must still have felt I had a little face worth seeing, because that summer that I turned six my portrait was painted by gifted artist Theodore Lukits. Mama Lee picked me up at my parents' home in Hollywood and drove me to the afternoon "sittings" at Lukits' Normandie Avenue studio. Jack was away, accompanying the Winslows to their longtime summer cottage at Alexandria Bay. They would not return until the bass fishing season was over in September. I was the first child Mr. Lukits had ever attempted to paint. I remember having to sit "very still." I could talk, but not move my head nor body.

Known for his watercolors and oils of the desert, Lukits was venturing into Hollywood portraiture and would paint the wife of director Billy Wilder soon thereafter. Back In Chicago, where, as a young man, he had attended the Art Institute, actress Theda Bara had encouraged him to move out west. She was pleased with the portrait he had painted of her, and felt other Hollywood celebrities might want to use his talent to enhance their images. They did, and among them were Ray Milland, Delores del Rio and William Wyler.

About the time Harry Cohn moved out of the home on Fremont Place, Aunt Rose ventured deeply into the world of the arts in Los Angeles. Remembering how she had sponsored high-society musicales in her New York City days, as the former wife of a high-powered attorney there, she became particularly interested in promoting opera and the symphony, becoming close friends with many members of the orchestra. Among them she knew Mr. and Mrs. Joseph Levy, who were sponsoring a child violin protégé, Sandra Berkova. Though I could barely stay awake during the evening performances, Aunt Rose took me along to hear the young violinist, who was then about my age. Sandra was such a little virtuoso that she would make two transcontinental concert tours before she was eleven.

Aunt Rose was shorter than, yet greatly resembled, her sister Tillie, but their manner of dress was totally different. Whereas Mommie Winslow was always well groomed, she dressed with a marked restraint. She used to admonish me, all the years I was growing up, "Laura June, dress in such a way that people will remember that you looked good, but they won't quite be able to remember exactly what you were wearing." Aunt Rose, on the other hand, dressed with a memorable flash and flair. She wore platform high heels with ankle straps. Her dresses were low cut, front and back, and made of shiny fabrics like taffeta. And she was loaded with jewels, especially two

I remember. She had an enormous square-cut diamond, about twenty-five carats, for her left hand. A brooch made of cascading rubies, emeralds and diamonds was always on her dress near the neckline. Later, when I was a teenager, I would be given her cast-off silver and white fox jackets.

George Gershwin died of a brain tumor the summer of 1937. I remember hearing on the radio, time and again, the next-to-the last song he composed, "Love Walked In," and then hearing later on a news broadcast that he had died. Aunt Rose took me to the Hollywood Bowl for a memorial concert held in his honor in September. The Winslows had not yet returned from their three-month sojourn in the East. When I accompanied Aunt Rose, I always preferred the outdoor concerts to the indoor ones held at the Wilshire-Ebell, or the Philharmonic Auditorium downtown, just across from Pershing Square.

Because the Winslows had lived in New York City till they passed their silver wedding anniversary, I was to begin to meet a succession of their friends who visited from the east coast. Among them were Hattie Silverman, Millie and Max Gordon and Saul and Bonnie Bornstein. I loved "Aunt Hattie" from the moment I met that warm-hearted redheaded matron. She was the widow of the founder and publisher of *Variety*, Sime Silverman. He had died at the Ambassador Hotel several years before, and the last friends to see him before his late-evening death were Tillie and Max. They visited Groman's Mortuary before his body was shipped East for burial. Mommie Winslow told me Sime was laid out for viewing, but the funeral director had slicked back the unruly shock of hair that always graced his brow. "Give me a comb," she asked the mortuary attendant. "Sime needs to go home like he always looked in life." And she brought back his customary hair-style.

In 1919, the Silvermans and the Winslows had bought side-by-side summer cottages on the St. Lawrence River, west of the village of Alexandria Bay, looking out on the famed resort area. I wouldn't call them cottages for they were full-sized homes. Here the two couples had retreated from the stifling heat and humidity of summers in New York City. They would be neighbors like this for over twenty years. When the Winslows returned from their three months in the Thousand Islands, they brought Aunt Hattie with

Aunt Hattie Silverman and Daddy Max cavorting on the lawn next to the Winslows' cottage.

them. She had raised a now grown married son, so she knew how to get on a child's level for a serious conversation.

On May 12, 1937, the English Duke of York, and his wife Elizabeth were crowned King and Queen of the British Empire. That was the era when it was true: "The sun never sets on the British Empire." Little girls everywhere, myself included, wanted to be like the little Princesses, Elizabeth (now Queen Elizabeth II), and Margaret Rose, about whom newspapers wrote profusely. One night, during her stay at the Chateau, Aunt Hattie asked Mommie Winslow if I might come to her apartment and spend the night with her. Her suite looked out across a stretch of lawn to where the Winslows' apartment was located one floor down. She had twin beds so we slept in the same room.

In the morning, Aunt Hattie had already dressed and was helping me to get ready for the day. I sat on the side of the bed telling her I wished I were a princess, like little Elizabeth. Hattie was kneeling on the floor, tying my shoelaces for me, since I had not mastered that skill as yet. "Oh, no, Laura June, don't wish for that! Why, if you were a little princess, even when you grew up, people would have to be putting on and tying your shoes, like I am doing now. How would you like that? I don't think so!" If nothing else, Aunt Hattie was a realist of the first order, and I didn't mind her disillusioning me.

One Saturday afternoon, Daddy Max took me to see the first feature length Disney film, *Snow White and the Seven Dwarfs*. Irving Berlin, Inc. owned the copyrights for the musical score. The precursors of the future Disneyland and Disney World characters peopled the entranceway to the Carthay Circle Theater. These life-sized brilliantly costumed dwarfs frightened me, and I clung tightly to Daddy Max's hand, and even more so, when the Wicked Step-mother morphed into the Ugly Witch at the climax of the animated film. Sixty-seven years later, I am still thrilled by hearing the musical score for that classic.

Sometime that year of 1937 I accompanied my middle brother to radio station KFWB. An old yellowed newspaper clipping says that I had worked on radio, but about that I have no memory. The news item appeared in November 1937 because my oil portrait had been finished by artist Lukits, in the early fall. He scheduled two showings or "unveilings," as they were called. The first was in his Normandie Avenue studio, and the second was held at the Hollywood Women's Club, which was then located near La Brea Avenue on Hollywood Boulevard. The guest lists included the parents of my playmates, the Frank Capras and Maurice Reingolds, Uncle Guy and Aunt Brownie Kibbee, as well as Harold Lloyd, the film comic who had made fame and fortune at Hal Roach's studio. What I recall about the two evenings was that a "noted harpist," Mary Frances Schreiber, filled the air with music, and there were good things to eat, like little sandwiches and cookies and punch. Later, the portrait would hang in the Bertram Newhouse Galleries of the Beverly-Wilshire Hotel. Today it hangs on the eleventh floor of the downtown Los Angeles Jonathan Club, a gift of Mr. Lukits before his death.

That busy fall of 1937 I was to have my "Big Moment" in the *Little Rascals* two-reel production of the *Our Gang Follies of 1938*. I was selected to be one of the four little girls who "went bananas" when sailor-clad "Alfalfa" croons to them. Gloria Hurst, Darla Hood, and another girl and I were dressed in hula skirts, little flowered halter tops, a lei around our

The Lukits oil painting of Laura June.

necks and grass anklets just above our ballet-slippered feet. I am the last of the little ladies to tiptoe onstage in the Rascals' cellar-type theater and seat myself near the crooning "Alfalfa." At the end of his song, the camera moves to me, where adoringly I look at the crooner, and lift my shoulders in a big visual sigh of adoration. It's not what Andy Warhol would characterize as my "Fifteen minutes of fame," but more like my five minutes of fame!

At the end of the movie, the whole ensemble of hula girls and their sailor partners take the clubhouse stage and sing farewell to the audience of children and movie-goers. There I am, feet planted firmly apart, in contrast to the other girls with their little feet daintily together. I hadn't learned the lyrics well, so the viewer can see me looking to the others for what to do or what to sing next. The camera quickly moves from my ineptitude and focuses on the more polished child performers. Ah, but I could effect a wonderful sigh, and I must have been picked for that!

There is a dream sequence in the film, supposedly taking place in "Club Spanky," a prototype of the nightclub kids would like to have. Inside the cabaret are a lot of children, "dressed to the nines," eating and dancing. I remember sitting at one of the tables, staring at what was supposed to be an ice cream sundae set in front of me. The great artifice of show business is that it can make balls of mashed potatoes look like scoops of ice cream. Real ice cream would have melted in seconds under the hot studio lights. Today on video, I can see the back of myself, with my long curls, dance by when Darla and "Alfalfa" were in a scene, in which she brags about her show business success. This last of the Hal Roach two-reelers was released just before Christmas 1937.

That too was a memorable Christmas. I did not receive the Princess Elizabeth Doll with its tiny tiara I so longed for, but Chico Marx gave me my first camera. It was not one of the old Kodak box cameras but a sleek little model of molded black plastic. I would use that loving gift for the next fifteen years. And there were beautiful clothes, and books, and lots of Disney-ware items, — soaps, dusting powder, etc., all with the *Snow White and the Seven Dwarfs* motif. Old Walt was, from his beginnings, always the entrepreneur and salesman!

1938 would be a special year I would never forget. For one thing, it would be the last year the Williams family would live in the fine old Victorian mansion on Stanley Street. The lot the two-story mansion occupied was nearly a half-acre, and trapezoidal in shape. The lot had two corners where perpendicular lines met, the northwestern and northeastern. But the Red Car streetcar line abutted its diagonal southern boundary, crossing Stanley Street at a forty-five degree angle. The five-bedroom house sat to one side of the lot, leaving a huge backyard, in contrast to a narrow portion of lot toward the street. Our middle brother, Roger, was an athlete, signing up for track, so Dad helped him install a sawdust pit for pole-vaulting with an earthen runway where he could build up speed before he attempted the vault.

There was a huge jacaranda tree, which came in bloom with its blue-lilac blossoms just in time to mark my birthday each year. Dad hung a swing from one of its branches, where I spent a lot of time playing make-believe, all by myself, sitting in that swing. During first grade I met another friend from Gardner Street School, Deborah Marshall. She lived a couple of blocks west, and after Grandmother walked me there and back a couple of times I was trusted to go visit her all by myself. Also I could walk up Stanley Street almost to Sunset Boulevard and take a few piano lessons from the mother of Esther Worthy. But I was no better at piano than I had been at tap-dancing, so the lessons were abandoned.

The interior of the house was fairly well preserved. The living and dining rooms had the sculpted tin ceilings so popular at the turn-of-the-century, and they were high. The living room had once held a pipe organ, and though that instrument was long gone, the gilded pipes remained on one wall. There were sliding doors between the living room and the dining room. And the one bathroom in the house held a toilet with a water-tank above. When a flush was desired, you pulled a chain suspended from the tank. Gravity did the rest.

One day I was home with Grandmother. The hot-water tank was not automatic as today's models are. Pressure built up in the tank and forced water backwards through pipes laid from the street to the house. Grandmother and I watched as a geyser of hot water spurted upwards in our front yard. I did not understand the gravity of the situation and laughed hysterically. As usual, my mother was not pleased. Grandmother was scolded as well, and more and more I wanted to get out of the way, be somewhere else, so Mother wouldn't talk to me that way or look at me with such scorn.

If I weren't waiting for Jack to come and call for me, taking me to be with the Winslows at the Chateau, I was counting the hours till the

Taken on a weekend with Mama Lee and Daddy Carl.

weekend came and Mama Lee and Daddy Carl would call for me. My two days with them would be filled with simple pleasures, good food, lots of music, and sometimes surprises, like the time they took me along with them by water-taxi from the Redondo Beach Pier to the gambling ship, the *S.S. Rex*, just outside the three-mile limit. We went at night, and the steamship shone brightly, as we approached it, and were taken aboard. If Lee and Carl went to a card party, I went along and the hostess would always have a bed for me to stretch out upon when I got weary. I would fall asleep to the soft lulling sound of adult laughter and quiet talk. Or maybe we would go to a new kind of venue that was called a drive-in movie, where a family sat in their car, mounted a speaker in the vehicle and watched the film on a huge screen. Whatever was new and different piqued the interest of my first foster-parents!

Carl was using his talents for inventing, and developed the steering-wheel knob sold by the Hope Manufacturing Company in downtown Los Angeles. Lee, without me to care for on a day-to-day basis, had taken up real estate sales. Together they began the custom of purchasing a new car every year. The Winslows did the same. After Jack would send the Winslows off on the Super Chief for Chicago each June, he would take a bus to Detroit, and there pick up a new model of Dodge or Buick, and break in the new vehicle by driving it to the Thousand Islands, where it would be used during the summer. Come September 15, when the bass fishing season ended on the St. Lawrence River, the Winslows would close up their summer home and then spend a few days or a week in New York City, before leaving for home in California. That interlude would allow for Jack to drive the car back across the country from upstate New York to California. Then he would meet them at the Santa Fe station in Pasadena. Sometimes I was with him for their train departures and arrivals.

In late May of 1938, Hal Roach sold the entire *Our Gang* company to M-G-M. That meant that the last two episodes of the Little Rascals in which I would appear were shot at the huge Metro complex in Culver City. The first one was called *Party Fever*. I have a hand-out "glossy" which shows me sitting next to Darwood "Waldo" Kaye in an outdoor scene on Metro's back lot. Tommy "Butch" Bond sits on the other side of "Waldo." "Alfalfa" is seen in a mock hot-air balloon tethered in the hands of "Buckwheat."

The last *Our Gang* episode I remember being in, *Aladdin's Lantern*, was shot on a huge Metro sound stage, where the Rascals' old clubhouse with its audience area and stage were reconstituted. I was to appear as part of the audience, and not a participant onstage this time. One of "Alfalfa's" off-screen traits was humiliating other cast members and playing pranks on the set, sometimes causing costly delays. In a break between "takes," "Alfalfa" must have noticed that I liked looking at his real-life older brother Harold Switzer. The previous year Harold had stood next to me in the final scene of the *Our Gang Follies of 1938*. "Alfalfa" asked me, "Do you like my brother?" I nodded shyly, then "Alfalfa" shouted out so all the cast and crew could hear, "Harold, see that girl in the green dress? She likes you!" I was so embarrassed, that I looked down the bench where I was seated, and pointed to another girl, also wearing a green dress that day.

"Not me, it's her," I said. I really didn't like attention being paid to me that way. One day when I went to the Saturday matinee at the Vista Theater on Sunset Boulevard, the *Our Gang Follies of 1938* was one of the shorts seen between a double feature. As I emerged from the theater, other children pointed at me and said, "You were in that movie, weren't you?" Again I denied being the one they had seen sighing over "Alfalfa's" crooning. I did not want to be seen as "different." Though I did not know the meaning of the word, it was obvious I did not enjoy the status of a "celebrity!"

Sometime during the filming of those two Rascal episodes, Mother and I went to the M-G-M commissary for the rare treat of a hot meal during the shooting day. It was soup we had, but no matter, who should cross my path as we went to our table to eat? It was no less than Clark Gable! And he was as handsome in real life as he was in all the movies I had seen with Mama Lee and Daddy Carl on my weekend visits. Even a seven-year-old found his dark good looks and beaming smile quite wonderful to behold!

Filmmaking is a tedious process for all concerned, cast and crew. The long breaks between takes, when lighting and sound adjustments were being arranged, made for boredom if the director didn't need your services at the moment. What I frequently saw on movie-sets, even those where there were lots of children, were grips and gaffers and members of the crew down on the soundstage floor, on their knees, in a small circle, shooting craps.

Oh, yes, gambling was commonplace, even with studio bosses! In later years Jack related to me how Daddy Max was commandeered by studio-head Harry Cohn to take cash pay-outs from his gambling losses to dark little corners of Hollywood. Jack had to drive him there. Though Max liked cards and poker as well as anybody, —he had once won a single pot of $3200.00 in a game with Sime Silverman, — he did not relish the furtive, underworld aspect of Cohn's gambling exploits. Daddy Max did not like being his brother-in-law's errand-boy to the seamier side of Los Angeles life in the 1930's.

I turned seven, my sister Joyce took her first steps holding a birthday balloon on a stick, and my brother Chester graduated from Hollywood High in June of 1938. His high school always held their summer commencement exercises in the Hollywood Bowl. Attending that event was for me just the first of exciting events to transpire that summer.

Mommie Winslow announced, around the time of my birthday, that she and Daddy Max were not going east to the Thousand Islands for their usual three-month fishing vacation. I was told about a huge suspension bridge that was just being completed, just a few miles west of the Winslow's summer home in St. Lawrence Park. The bridge would join the mainland of upstate New York to Grindstone Island. Another bridge, further north, would make Ontario, Canada, accessible. The river would not be so good for fishing that summer of 1938.

Mommie Winslow also insisted that Daddy Max was very busy at the studio and couldn't get away to accompany us, — she and myself, and Jack, — on a huge motor tour of California. Yes, he was busy, not heading the music department, as he had been, for the past five years, but rather cleaning out his desk and office at Columbia Pictures. Except for the five pictures with opera star Grace Moore, whose production Daddy Max had overseen, Harry Cohn had not embraced the idea of more money being spent on musicals at Columbia. Max had wanted to do the life of various composers, such as Chopin, but Cohn wouldn't even consider that idea until after Max had died. When I later saw Chopin's life depicted on the screen in Columbia's *A Song To Remember*, Mommie Winslow would tell me, "This was Daddy Max's dream, to produce this movie!" As soon as that film was eventually released, she sent me to the Pantages Theater, a few blocks from the Chateau, to take in an afternoon matinee performance!

Before Daddy Max left Columbia Pictures, Jack took him out to the airport to meet his partner, Irving Berlin, flying out to "the Coast," to discuss business of an extremely important nature. The two men took a long drive, then had lunch, finally leaving the car in front of Columbia to walk up and down Gower Street, talking with dramatic gestures. Jack couldn't figure out their animated topic. Maybe the discussion centered on their not-to- be-trusted third partner, Saul Bornstein, maybe it was the wily Harry Cohn, whose employ Max was about to leave. Maybe it was Berlin's problems with Daryl Zanuck. Whatever the problem up for discussion, Winslow and Berlin relied on each other's point of view and advice.

I didn't help the tense situation between Daddy Max and Uncle Harry Cohn, either. Mommie Winslow had just taught me to make telephone calls. I would practice, when visiting her, dialing out on their private phone. Sometimes I would use the "house phone," as I was learning to ask the hotel telephone operator to place a call to friends and family of the Winslows. Often I called Daddy Max at his office at Columbia, just to ask him when Jack was to pick him up at the studio. But one day I was home on Stanley Street, and I thought I would call Uncle Harry at Columbia. The studio operator recognized my voice, and hesitated to put me through, but finally relented. "Who is this?" Harry roared into the phone. I gave my name, and he slammed down the receiver. Shortly thereafter, he told Max and Tillie, "Don't ever let that child call here again. I don't talk to children!"

Though they lived apart, and were actually separated, tension was growing between Aunt Rose and Uncle Harry Cohn. He had a strong romantic liaison with a young Columbia starlet, Joan Perry, but he objected to attention being paid to Aunt Rose by the musical luminaries, — violinists, pianists, opera singers, — who came to Los Angeles to perform. She entertained many of them and introduced them to important show business people. I remember going often to the Fremont Place home with Mommie Winslow as she tried to calm and comfort Aunt Rose after the latter would have received a withering phone call from her estranged husband. Max, working at Columbia for Harry Cohn, and Tillie, being Rose Cohn's sister, made for great awkwardness. Besides, Daddy Max was tiring of the role of being a messenger for his brother-in-law to underworld gambling and racket figures. Daddy Max would go fishing that summer for new creative endeavors, far from the studio on Gower Street, and his studio boss's tyrannical attitudes and antics.

School was out mid-June and there was a flurry of shopping for me, —for play-clothes and traveling wear, summer shoes, and sweaters. Mommie Winslow bought me two of everything, so that, while on the trip, I could wear one outfit while the other would be cleaned by the hotel laundry, wherever we stopped.

Our odyssey began in early July, our first destination, Yosemite National Park. Jack headed the big black Buick north of Los Angeles, taking the Ridge Route to Bakersfield where we spent the first night. In the early afternoon the next day, we stopped in Fresno for a cool drink, and I saw my first sight of gypsies, sauntering on the sidewalk, wearing long, colorful skirts, lots of beads and bandanas. I was fascinated, and a little frightened, for I had heard tales of gypsies stealing children. As nightfall approached, we reached the ancient Wawona Hotel, where we spent our first night in the Sierra Nevadas.

Next morning, we would enter Yosemite by the southern route. Suddenly you emerge from a tunnel, and there before you is a sight that can only be called breathtaking! The whole glacial valley lies before you, El Capitan off to the left, and majestic Half Dome straight ahead, a little to the right. We did not linger long to take in this view, but drove the winding valley road to the Ahwahnee Hotel. Mommie Winslow had arranged for us to have one of the cottages on the wooded grounds of the hotel. She and I would have our own bedroom and bath, and Jack would have his. In the mornings we would walk to the enormous hotel dining room to have our breakfast, but dinner, that was a different matter. We had our dinner served out on the stone terrace outside the dining room. There, promptly at nine p.m., we could hear the park ranger, stationed at Camp Curry, beneath Glacier Point, send his echoing cry upwards: "Let the fire fall!" At this signal, men, atop Glacier Point, three thousand feet above the valley floor, would push burning coals, with their long rakes, over the edge of the cliff. And for a few seconds, a fall of burning embers would rival the waterfalls so famous in Yosemite. Once seen, it is a sight never to be forgotten, indelibly imprinted in memory.

We stayed at the Ahwahnee for a week. In the mornings Jack and I swam in the chill waters of the Merced River, then after lunch and a nap, we explored the whole area, seeing both groves of the ancient *Sequoia Gigantea*, the fat giant redwoods of California, or driving to Glacier Point, or viewing the many waterfalls, then in full plumage. On the road to Glacier Point, where there was a small lodge, we saw a mother bear with her two small cubs by the roadside. When we reached the lodge, high atop the valley, we saw the workmen turning and raking the coals, preparing for the fire fall a few hours later. The view of the "high country" from Glacier Point is understated, even if you use the word "spectacular" to describe it! Spread, wherever you can see, is what John Muir termed his beloved Sierras, "The Range of Light."

Myself, beside the Merced River at Yosemite.

I call on this, my first experience and memory of the beauty of Yosemite, even to this day, while sitting in the dental chair, when I need to visualize something peaceful. And I created a structured visualization from this memory all during twenty radiation treatments for breast cancer fifteen years ago. Yosemite, is for me, my Shangri-la!

Our threesome left Yosemite by the western route, down the winding road that paralleled the old train route to El Portal. We spent the night at a lovely old hotel in Merced, then headed back to Los Angeles the next day. So engrossed was Mommie Winslow by the beauty of an undiscovered California landscape, she decided that there should be a longer, more extensive tour of California. We would make it, even if Daddy Max could not "get away" from the studio. There were really two reasons for his not being with us. Years later, Mommie Winslow told me he was afraid of heights, and when she described to him the beautiful mountain drives, he would turn pale.

The second reason he did not join our entourage was because he was going into an agency partnership with his old poker-playing friend from New York City, Jack Curtis, and with an old friend from music-publishing days, Bobby Crawford. They would be front-page news in the *Hollywood Reporter*: "In this new setup of Crawford, Curtis and Winslow, Max will devote most of his attention to stories and writers. Quite a combination those three boys, and they should do mighty well for themselves and for this picture industry. They will bring an honesty and integrity to the general agency business."

Mother unpacked, washed and ironed all my clothes while I went off to spend a few days with Mama Lee and Daddy Carl, since the projected tour of California was going to be longer than our initial trip. Hollywood Park Race Track had just opened, so the three of us went to spend two days at the races. I liked seeing the horses, but what interested me most was a large pond in the grassy oval surrounded by the track. On the pond were geese, and a girl tended them, dressed as a shepherdess. She was dubbed "The Goose Girl." With binoculars, I would follow her movements and not those of the speeding horses.

At the track with us were some members of the Candreva family. Six brothers in the family had been a sextet of trumpeters on the old vaudeville circuit, and could tell stories of being on the bill with Bing Crosby in the 1920s. But with vaudeville being virtually dead, some of them had joined the orchestras of various movie studios. For years, at KFI, the NBC radio station in Los Angeles, the trumpeters heralded the nightly ten o'clock news with a little recorded trumpet fanfare. Now the brothers found musical jobs wherever they could.

Then it was time for our second expedition to explore the Golden State. We headed north from the San Fernando Valley along the mountainous Newhall and Saugus road that led past what would become the desert towns of Palmdale and Lancaster. In one day we drove only as far as Mojave, and had to spend the night there. Nowadays my husband and I traverse this same area in one and a half hours via modern freeways. Our next stopover would be the Winnedumah Hotel in Independence, on the backside of the Sierra Nevada mountains. The following day we reached our destination,

Lake Tahoe, but we had to spend that first night on the eastern shore, the Nevada side of that jewel-like lake. On the fourth day since we departed, we would settle down at the now-defunct Tahoe Tavern Hotel. We made a quick side-trip to Reno en route to have a new key made for the trunk in which Mommie Winslow had inadvertently locked our key.

The fanfare-playing Candreva Bothers.

For years after, the three of us would joke about that excursion. Reno was a rough town, still full of miners, gamblers and divorce seekers. (Las Vegas was hardly on the map at that time.) We needed a cool drink, so handsome, clean-cut, twenty-three year-old Jack strolled into a bar. Convenience stores like 7-11 were unknown. "What'll it be?" asked the burly barkeep.

Jack feigning a roughness so unlike him, snarled, "Gimme three Seven-Ups!" and pounded his fist on the bar. Afterwards we got our key made, and eventually our trunk unpacked in time for a dressy dinner in the posh grand dining room of the Tavern. An orchestra was playing Irving Berlin's music, for the movie, *Alexander's Ragtime Band*, had just opened across the country. Night after night we would eat dinner, listening to the music Daddy Max's "discovery" had brought to the world!

We took a speedboat cruise all over the lake, and drove its circumference on another day, and of course, Jack and I swam each morning. Mommie Winslow had very fair skin and protected herself against the sun's rays by wearing wide-brimmed hats and long sleeved dresses. She never went near the water. One day when we were on the Nevada side of the Lake, she gave me a quarter to play a slot machine, and I hit the jackpot, with a noisy cascade of quarters for my winnings.

We took two days to reach the San Francisco Bay area, for Jack had a friend he wanted to look up in the town of Lincoln, northeast of Sacramento. Finally we reached San Francisco's St. Francis Hotel on Union Square. I was so tired that first night that Mommie Winslow ordered a "Room Service" tray for me, before she bedded me down for the night. Whenever I taste honey dew melon now, I am suddenly transported to the St. Francis, and my first taste of it in a bowl of melon-balls. We had nearly a week wandering the Bay Area, sightseeing the Seal Rocks, Coit Tower, Chinatown and Fisherman's Wharf, where we ate dinner at the restaurant of Joe diMaggio's family. One day we crossed the Bay to explore the campus of the University of California in Berkeley. Little did I know that ten years later I would enter that campus as a freshman. Perhaps a seed had been planted by Mommie Winslow that sunny long-ago day.

The spectacular Golden Gate Bridge and the two-span Bay Bridge were only recently completed, and as we drove over the latter, we could see the workmen preparing the site for the Golden Gate International Exposition, which would open the summer of 1939. A flatlands had been created adjacent to Yerba Buena Island through which the bridge tunnel ran. This area would be dubbed "Treasure Island" for the forthcoming exposition.

August 10 we completed our stay in San Francisco by having lunch at the famed Palace Hotel, where President Warren G. Harding had died of a heart attack in 1923, and the site for my future high school graduating class's senior breakfast. Little did I know, that I would one day live for five years in the city we were now leaving!

Our circuit took us next to the Monterey Bay crescent, a hundred miles south of "The City." Here we stayed at the old Del Monte Hotel, now a postgraduate school for U.S. Navy officers. I remember the beautiful trees and gardens Mommie Winslow and I strolled. We went into Monterey proper to see the Cannery Row made famous by author John Steinbeck and had a meal in Pacific Grove, retirement community of the West's very rich.

Next stop would be a few days' stay in Carmel, reached by Jack's navigating the Seventeen Mile Drive near Pebble Beach. We stayed in a cottage at the Carmel Highlands Inn, and mornings Jack and I would go to the beach, usually shrouded in fog. One afternoon we went to Mission Carmel and stood by the tomb of Father Junipero Serra, Franciscan founder of Spanish California's string of missions along the old El Camino Real. One evening we went to a silent movie, "The Sheik," with Rudolph Valentino, and another night saw the newer movie, "The Girl of the Golden West," starring Jeanette Mac Donald and Nelson Eddy.

Our trio was now on the home stretch of our journey. Down scenic Highway 1 we would take a winding trail southward, Jack hugging the cliffs above the ocean far below. Past San Simeon and the Hearst Castle, perched high on its mountaintop, we moved on to Morro Bay. There would be two more nights on the road, but they are vague in memory, except that we lingered for a night and a day in Santa Barbara. Then we were home in Hollywood, and the map I carry in my head had greatly expanded to include a map of the better part of the state of California. Two years later, when I would be in Grade Four, when California children routinely study the establishment of the Missions of California, and learn of the California gold rush, I would have a mental backdrop against which to imagine those events.

Mommie Winslow and Daddy Max would hear from a grief-stricken Frank and Lu Capra shortly after our return to Los Angeles. Their beloved second son, Johnny, had died from complications of a tonsillectomy at Children's Hospital, the site of my own little brother's demise. The day of Johnny's funeral, Jack picked me up from Stanley Street and whisked me out to the Capra's Malibu Colony home, where I spent the day, playing with four-year-old Frankie, Junior. Some adult was there to watch over us as we played on the sand by the sea or in the beach house. I remember how Mommie Winslow indicated I was just to spend the day with Frankie until late afternoon when Jack would call for me and take me back to Hollywood. Frankie had a baby sister but she was too little to companion him that sad day in his young life.

In 1938, radio and newspapers described a killer hurricane that hit the East Coast on September 21. Although I never heard them discuss it, I knew Mommie Winslow and Daddy Max were glad they had forsaken their usual summer trip to the Thousand Islands that always ended with a mid-September visit to New York City.

My brother Chester began to study art with Ted Lukits that fall, and he also took a job retouching photos for a Hollywood Boulevard photographer whom we came to call "The Mad Russian." He it was who posed me for my favorite childhood photo. Photos of my little face must have made the rounds in Hollywood, for I auditioned for several parts in movies, in none of which I would be cast. One such film was David O. Selznick's block-buster, *Gone With the Wind*. Mother accompanied me out to the Selznick Production Center near Metro-Goldwyn-Mayer and the Hal Roach Studio I knew so well. I said a few lines for the casting people, along with dozens of other little girls, all of us vying for the part of Scarlett and Rhett Butler's little girl Bonnie. My fair hair and skin were not what was wanted. I could not have been the daughter of brunette Vivien Leigh and "tall, dark and handsome" Clark Gable.

I also read for Daddy Max at his agency office out in Beverly Hills. With others present, he explained the storyline, and asked me if I could think of something really, really sad to evoke tears. Strange to tell, I conjured up the death of my Mother, — not the death of Mommie Winslow or Mama

Lee, — which brought me to tears. Many years later, in therapy, I would realize that I could become sad, very sad as a child, mourning a relationship that had never come into being. At some level, I was grieving the antipathy

My favorite childhood photo.

of my Mother toward me and mine toward her. She merely "endured" my presence in her life, and there was never any bonding between us. But at age seven, how could I understand that? Thinking of her death somehow produced the needed tears for reading the scene.

I remember hearing Kate Smith sing an Irving Berlin song in November of 1938. Daddy Max and Mommie Winslow called me into Daddy Max's bedroom, where we usually listened to evening radio programs after we had eaten dinner in the tiny dining room. In that spacious bedroom, more like a sitting room, he was teaching me to play solitaire, and sometimes we played rummy there. "Listen to this, Laura June. Isn't it beautiful? This song is very special," Daddy Max beamed with approval. And it was! The song was "God Bless America," and by the next year, my class at school was singing the whole song, verse and refrain.

That fall, when I was in second grade, I missed the teaching of subtraction in school. Either Daddy Max or Uncle Guy Kibbee arranged for me to be in a movie scene out at Warner's Studio. A family, of which I was supposed to be the youngest member, was eating breakfast as the scene unfolded. Of course, as usual, Mother and I went to the studio in the dark of the morning, and I had not had sufficient to eat at such an early hour. Lo, and behold, instead of fake food, like mashed potatoes standing in for ice cream, a la the *Little Rascals*, there was real edible food on the table. There was Grape-Nuts cereal and real cream! "Take one." I began to eat silently while the adults in the scene said their lines. The director said, "Cut." I continued to eat, though all dramatic action had ceased for the moment. "Take two," and I relished the treat of real cream. Another "Cut," and I proceeded to finish off the bowl of cereal. When "Take three" was announced, I was full and just sat there, unable to take another bite, or even force myself to look like I was hungry and eating. The director was furious and yelled at me. Obviously, I was not to be seen in that movie, nor work at Warner Brothers again.

Each year, Max Gordon, Broadway producer, and his beautiful wife Millie, would come to California, either to vacation or work on a picture. Daddy Max and "Uncle Max" had been friends in New York City before the Winslows moved west in 1933. Uncle Max was one of Broadway's great producers, at one time having four dramatic hits running simultaneously on "The Great White Way." He it was who found a very funny vaudeville comedian at the Palace Theater, featured him in the early thirties musical, *Roberta*, and thus helped to give the world the great comic talent of Bob Hope. Now Uncle Max wanted to try his hand at moviemaking, so in December of 1938, he and "Aunt Millie" came west just before Christmas, and I was taken to meet the couple at the Beverly-Wilshire Hotel. I was to see a lot of them the following year.

But it was Christmas, our last Christmas in the old mansion with the high metal ceilings, and we were to move before the end of December. After four full years, the bank that had rented my parents the property, found a buyer for the odd-shaped lot and Victorian "White Elephant" house. The Depression had put a damper on couples having big families of children such as ours. I once heard it said that the year in which I was born, 1931, produced the lowest birth rate in United States history, thus many of my classmates through the years were "only children." Mother and Dad had a hard time finding a big enough house for the eight of us, and at a price Dad could afford on his meager wages. Work was still hard to find! For a few months we even took in a "roomer," – "The Mad Russian" photographer, whom brother Chester assisted in his Hollywood Boulevard photo studio.

The Williamses, along with Grandmother Reese, moved to 1950 Wilton Place, another Victorian home, still occupied to this day. I was thrilled because the big home was just blocks from the Chateau and I could walk to Mommie Winslow's and Daddy Max's apartment, and Jack wouldn't have to call for me at school anymore. In fact, the new school, Chermoya Avenue School, was located just diagonally from the Chateau on Franklin Avenue. The winter and spring of 1939 I became like the famous literary "Eloise" who knew every corner of the New York Plaza Hotel. I spent so much time with Mommie Winslow that she often allowed me to explore the grounds and the building at will. I rode the elevator to the high terrace that looks out on all of Hollywood, wandered the gardens, particularly the path by the stream, and often stopped to watch grown-ups playing tennis in the court just adjacent to Mommie Winslow's bedroom.

I had the whole Chateau as a kind of backdrop for my solitary dramatic play. The staff became accustomed to my comings and goings even though I was the only child in the building. I remember I met the concierge, who occupied a small apartment near the front desk. She was Eleanor Otis, and she recognized me as a child with a vivid imagination. She frequently invited me into her quarters and asked me what I had been up to that particular day. The next Christmas she would give me my first writer's notebook, telling me, "Laura June, write down those stories you tell me." I treasured that little black leather binder for many decades after.

One time when I was using the elevator to go to the terrace, I met the character actress Spring Byington. She played the flustered mother in the Columbia movie, *You Can't Take It With You.* I had seen the movie, recognized her and was in great awe of being in her presence in that elevator. She asked me my name, and whom I was visiting, and I answered with all the politeness and decorum I could muster. As she left the elevator at her floor, she turned and said, "You have the nicest manners of any child I have ever seen!" Mommie Winslow had achieved with me what Alice Reingold had urged her to three years before! There is nothing like praise to enforce a positive behavior!

1939 was a big year in Hollywood, with the production of the blockbusters, *Gone with the Wind*, the *Wizard of Oz*, and also Frank Capra's *Mr. Smith Goes to Washington.* The latter two films I saw right away, but it would be years before I saw the classic film about the South and the Civil War, and realized the part for which I had auditioned had the little girl dying in a horseback riding accident.

It was also a big year for both coasts of the United States. North in San Francisco, where I had been the summer before, the Golden Gate International Exposition was due to open and entertain millions of visitors. On the east coast, the New York World's Fair would draw even bigger throngs of visitors. Mommie Winslow would be one of them. She left in mid-April, as she wanted to see everything before the summer heat and humidity, and then too, she and Daddy Max would go to the Thousand Islands for their usual summer of fishing, come June. The Winslows asked my parents if, in the summer of 1939, they could take me east to their summer cottage. My mother's answer was an emphatic "no." Both my parents feared the advent of an impending war in Europe and did not want me a continent's distance away should the war begin that summer, which indeed it did!

While Mommie Winslow toured the World's Fair she gathered all kinds of memorabilia for me, — a bracelet, photographs, postcards and albums commemorating the event. She also went to dinner at Rockefeller Center's Rainbow Room with Aunt Hattie Silverman and some other friends. Afterwards she sent to me, and Daddy Max, the large printed menu from the occasion. On it, Aunt Hattie scribbled this message for me: "You old stink pot – so you won't come to N.Y. Oh yeah! We'll get you yet. Never the more I love you." It would be twenty-seven years before I saw her cottage and Mommie Winslow's, side-by-side, at the edge of the Saint Lawrence River. She and the Winslows had so wanted me to come share their summer with them. On my dresser-top today is a little wooden keepsake box, hand-painted by Aunt Hattie and depicting the dock in front of the Winslow's cottage and a view of the river beyond. It is inscribed, "To Tillie Winslow, A memory that will never die, love, Hattie Silverman.....1950" I was not to see Aunt Hattie again, but she sent me a child's book about Benjamin Franklin, titled *Ben and Me*, which she purchased at the Watertown Book Store the following summer of 1940.

Daddy Max stayed behind in Hollywood, and the Max Gordons came to take up residence in a penthouse apartment at the Chateau. Now I went to visit Aunt Millie while I waited for Jack to go fetch Daddy Max from his Beverly Hills office. She was one of the most beautiful women I ever laid eyes upon. She had been a chorus girl, and an actress on both stage and in early movies, then filmed in New York. She and Uncle Max had never had children, but she was very comfortable with me. While Daddy Max was very "laid back" and easy-going, Uncle Max was one of the most intense show business people I ever met. Uncle Max was working on the film, "Abe Lincoln in Illinois," at the nearby R-K-O studio. He was also trying to put together a Jerome Kern musical to be staged that fall in New York. He was spreading himself too thin, and it showed. He was utterly stressed out. While Aunt Millie and I would visit quietly, he came home from the studio, pulled out a Murphy bed from the wall of the living room, and plopped down to unwind. After a rest or nap there, he and his wife would be ready to join Daddy Max and me for dinner at the Brown Derby nearby.

Mommie Winslow, on the shore of the St. Lawrence River.

There were two restaurants the Winslows frequented in Hollywood, —the Brown Derby on Vine Street and the Ivar House on Yucca Street. The Brown Derby was to Hollywood then what Sardi's was in New York City, a show business hang-out with great food. The booths were leather-lined and the Derby's walls hung with ink caricatures of the famous. Daddy Max liked to go there Thursday nights, as Thursday was always "The maid's day-off," and special dishes were prepared for Thursday diners. Sometimes on Tuesdays, we went to the Ivar House with its kimono-clad waitresses and delicious home-cooking. It didn't matter to me which restaurant was chosen, but you could see more celebrities at the Derby. Mommie Winslow held me to an iron-clad rule: I was never, never to ask a famous movie star for his or her autograph! It was enough that I would be introduced to them, and we could chat for a moment or two.

Over the years, in the course of these dinners at the Derby, I would be introduced to, among others, Jack Benny and Mary Livingston, Barbara Stanwyck and Robert Taylor (then married), George Jessel and Johnny Weissmuller, great Olympic swimmer and moviedom's Tarzan. Weissmuller insisted he give me his autograph, the only one I ever had. He wrote it on the back of a blank check. His wife, Lupe Velez, the "Mexican Spitfire" actress, was not with him, as they were divorcing. Later, my Dad would serve briefly as a substitute gardener for her Beverly Hills home.

Then it was June and I turned eight. Daddy Carl's steering-wheel knob production had been so profitable, he sold his interest in it, and he and Mama Lee purchased a new car. They were planning to be away the whole summer, visiting the South and all of Carl's many relatives, from Texas to Florida. Daddy Max was leaving for the East to join Tillie in the Thousand Islands. What I faced was a long summer without either set of foster-parents! Shirley Kibbee asked me to her birthday party, ten days after mine. As usual, the party was to be held at the Lakeside Golf Club at Toluca Lake, near Burbank. The invitation specified play-clothes and a swim-suit. I didn't know how to swim but I looked forward to being with Shirley and Aunt Brownie, who was always so warm and welcoming with me.

It is difficult to describe why I did what I did that day at the swimming party. I couldn't verbalize at home or to anybody how much that I was missing both sets of foster-parents. But the sense of loss was tremendous, even overwhelming. The long summer without them lay before me, as only the length of a summer can look to an eight-year-old, — endless! Aunt Brownie was so loving and gentle with me as well as with Shirley and Guy Jr. But her love would only be there for me for the length of the party that day. I was splashing around the shallow end of the pool with the other birthday guests, and suddenly I felt impelled to just walk out into the deep part of the pool, way over my head. It had something to do with wanting somebody to see what pain I was feeling. Later I would learn that children do get suicidal feelings, and in their own way, sometimes cry out for help when situations look hopeless to them. Of course, there was a lifeguard on duty, and he dived right in and brought me up to the water's surface before I swallowed too much water. Whether Aunt Brownie ever told my Mother of this incident I do not know.

Our family moved from Wilton Place after our six months lease was up. Our new home was a three-bedroom Spanish-style bungalow near the corner of Hollywood Boulevard. It was 1742 Laurel Canyon Boulevard, just where the Canyon begins its path through the Hollywood Hills. Behind the house was a barn-like structure where my three brothers could sleep and

Chester could do his painting and charcoal drawings for art class. There were eucalyptus trees, and I loved the smell of them. I had no friends, having just moved, and third grade with classmates was two and a half months in the future. I remember sitting on the front porch and counting the cars that went "over the hill" into the San Fernando Valley. Then I tried to identify all the cars that had license plates from other states. Sometimes I read what I could, although I was not yet "an independent reader," or I played with paper dolls. The most exciting thing that would happen was to sight "The hermit," a character clad in a sheet-like covering, walking down from the hills into Hollywood proper, leaning on a staff or tall walking stick. He had long white hair and an unkempt beard.

To my Mother's great credit, she recognized my boredom, if not my great loneliness, and she wrote to Grandma Shaffer, asking her if I could go to "The cabin" for a few weeks. Gram, who had taken in a "roomer," a graduate of the Civilian Conservation Corps, wrote back that she and Bill, who had a car, would call for me the next weekend. My bags were packed and off I went to Kagel Canyon. Gram let me run free all over the hills, as long as I checked in with her from time to time.

Kagel Canyon had a shallow stream running through it, with banks of clay, real clay. I found that fascinating. On the other side of the stream were the remnants of an old "road house" that had burned down, probably a "speakeasy" from Prohibition days. What was left was some stonework, and a chimney, and some evidence of a former dance floor. I used to go and stand there and imagine what it was like in "the old days," when Gram first moved to the canyon. Then I would go watch the C.C.C. boys clear an area for a new county park. Returning to the cabin for lunch, I'd have a stint at the player-piano, then take a nap on the sleeping porch.

Since the last time I had been to the cabin, someone had abandoned the carcass of an old 1920s sedan across the road. The seats had been removed. Grandma gave me some old wallpaper rolls, and then she made a flour paste, and together we papered the inside of the car. Now I had a most unusual playhouse, with "windows" of glass you could roll up and down. I spent hours in my little house.

As before, in the evenings we played cards or listened to the radio, though in the mountains, the reception was poor. About once a week the three of us went to Sunland or Tujunga or San Fernando to do the shopping for groceries. Occasionally there was a movie to see. Because I could not swim as yet, the pair never took me with them to "Pop's Willow Lake," so close at hand. Then the summer came to a close, and I returned to Hollywood during a very hot spell. Mother didn't let my brothers go to the one and only public "plunge" on La Cienega Boulevard because of her fear about their contracting polio. It was so hot that September that school was dismissed, once it started. I remember huge white thunderhead clouds like the ones so characteristic of Arizona or New Mexico. But the important thing was that both sets of foster-parents were returning to California, and we could resume the old routine, my triangle in space and time.

I was enrolled again at Gardner Street School, and now in the third grade. I walked each day to and from school along Hollywood Boulevard, the residential, west end of that famous street. One or two times I was allowed to take the "Red Car" streetcar from the stop nearest my school to Gower Street, where Mommie Winslow met me at the other end of that ride, and we walked up to the Chateau. I felt very big, being allowed to make the trip alone, at the age of eight.

At the end of September, I was requested to show up for an audition at the Charlie Chaplin Studios on the southeast corner of Sunset Boulevard and La Brea Avenue. Mother came to school and took me downtown to the Board of Education to get the customary work permit, but nothing developed from the audition. I was home sick with an earache and mastoiditis for three weeks that fall, but no doctor was called because I was supposedly a Christian Scientist. I could not keep food down except for pineapple juice, and my left ear drained constantly.

But I was well enough that fall when Halloween rolled around. Aunt Brownie Kibbee asked me to come out to the Valley and go trick-or-treating with Shirley. It was exciting because she drove us to the home of Bing Crosby, which looked like a Southern plantation manor home. As we approached the front porch, we saw a Negro butler, in full uniform, with a little table there, on which was a huge silver platter with a lid. When the butler lifted the lid, with tongs he gave us each a piece of fried chicken, the most unexpected of Halloween treats I ever received!

As November rolled around, and Mommie Winslow began her Christmas wrapping, she always asked Jack to take me with him out to Berverly Hills to call for Daddy Max at his agency office. One of the sweetest memories of our return drives to the Chateau was of my sitting next to Daddy Max, with his arm around me. And he would be singing to me, just as he had in his old song-plugging days. The songs were not the current hits we heard on the car radio, but the songs he had introduced to performers decades before, and my favorite and his began, "Oh, ma honey." He was serenading me with the song of Irving Berlin's that brought that great talent front and center in show business, "Alexander's Ragtime Band." It was that song that enabled Daddy Max to be called the "discoverer" of Irving Berlin's massive talent!

Dad finally got employment in Boulder City, Nevada, helping to put the finishing touches on the massive Boulder Dam Project. He came home only spasmodically, for it was a long bus ride back to Los Angeles. Dad's absence must have really upset my brother Paul, for he "ran away" with two other boys, all of them fourteen and in the ninth grade. One of the other boys was related to one of Daddy Max's associates, so there was much discussion about the boys' two or three day adventure, and retrieval and return by the police. I felt very sorry for Paul for the way Mother scolded him, it seemed to me endlessly!

The next time I was at Mama Lee's and Daddy Carl's, I went to have breakfast at Bertha McMahon's. As I dried the dishes for her, I told her about Paul's running away and how Mother scolded him and it bothered me. She, who was childless, replied, "That's too bad, Laura June, for the important thing is that your brother came home safely. Your mother should be grateful!" My conversation with Bertha was the first time I had discussed with anyone how cruel Mother could be. Bertha had never met her, so she was not reticent to tender her opinion of the situation.

Though Mommie Winslow had shopped for the makings of our family Thanksgiving and Christmas dinners for the previous three years, she had never taken me along for the shopping until I was eight. Jack took us to Balzar's on Larchmont Avenue, a very posh grocery store. There she selected every item of food that would appear on the holiday table, — turkey and ham, potatoes and vegetables, cranberries, rolls, butter, Black Forest Cake, and both a mince and pumpkin pie, even ice cream. We usually went grocery shopping on the day before the holiday, leaving just enough time for Balzar's to deliver the big boxes of food. That Thanksgiving our less opulent Kibbee cousins, the Milton Kibbee family, came to share the festive meal.

Milt was much younger than his brother Guy, and was used as a bit player in movies, three hundred and twenty four films, over a twenty-year career. He and his wife Lois had four children, one of whom went on to make a name for herself in television soap-operas. Their oldest daughter, Lois, appeared as Geraldine Saxon in *The Edge of Night*(1970-84) and as Elizabeth Sanders in *One Life to Live*(1986-88).

My middle brother Roger had a beautiful voice as well as great acting ability. Of the five of us children, he found the most plentiful work in movies and on radio. That particular fall he enrolled in a choir that was practicing to sing Christmas carols at the Broadway Hollywood Department Store, at famed Hollywood and Vine. I went along to the rehearsals out on the Sunset Strip, and was asked to sing along. When Christmas shopping kept the store open in the weeks before Christmas, I sometimes went with my brother and enjoyed singing with the choir. Clad in gold robes, high above the evening shoppers, we sang the traditional songs from the store's mezzanine.

Then Christmas was on the way, and when Dad's work was finished in Nevada, he came home and took me to see the Santa Claus parade on Hollywood Boulevard. Every night, except Sundays, after Thanksgiving, Santa Claus would come in a big float down Hollywood Boulevard, some movie-star celebrity riding with him, high on the float, where it looked like he was in his sleigh. Aunt Brownie called to say that Uncle Guy Kibbee would be riding with Santa and Shirley would sit between them. Dad and I went to the site of the end of the nightly spectacle, La Brea Avenue and

Hollywood Boulevard. There we waved frantically and called out to our step-cousins and Santa.

That Christmas I received from the Winslows a portable Decca record player that you had to wind up, and a variety of record albums of the old 78 rpm vintage. There was a *Babar the Elephant* album, an album of cowboy songs, an *Alice in Wonderland* collection, and the movie score from *Pinocchio* in one album. (Irving Berlin, Inc. owned this movie score also). Now I was no longer bored, and I was learning to read independently, going to the library with my brother Chester to bring books home. The decade in which I had been born was about to end. New Year's Day, listening to the Rose Parade on the radio, we would begin the "forties!"

With the coming of spring in 1940, I was called for work as an extra in the first of the three *Five Little Peppers* movies. The plots evolved from the novel of Margaret Sidney, and the movie would feature Edith Fellows, now a teenager, and Tommy Bond, both of whom had earlier been Little Rascals, like me, at the Hal Roach Studio. The film was shot in a soundstage down on Melrose Avenue, probably Paramount's. I had been to the *Ice Follies* and *Ice Capades* with Mommie Winslow and Daddy Max, in that same neighborhood, where there was an ice rink, perhaps the only such rink in all of Los Angeles at that time.

Mother accompanied me to the studio, and was not pleased with the outcome of casting for one of the parts. She said afterwards, "The only reason that little girl got the part was that her mother slept with the director."

I had not yet visited Roslyn, whose cousin was later that year to explain, to the two of us nine-year-olds, "the facts of life!" When the cousin described marital relations, I protested: "My father would never do that to my mother." Thus I was utterly in the dark when my Mother referred to some kind of "sleepover" at the director's home, and the mother of one of the cast was invited. It made absolutely no sense to me!

I was to appear in one more Five Little Peppers film, and this time, the scenes, for which I was needed, took place "on location," a term used to describe filming away from the big sound stages or the studio proper. A huge mansion, with a winding drive, set high atop Beverly Hills, was the site for the "location." We extras gathered at the studio, and were taken by buses, with the adults that always accompanied each child, up to that mountaintop. A caterer was hired to provide food for the noontime meal, since no one could leave the site to purchase any. And lo, and behold, this was the one and only time that I was present, that a schoolteacher was engaged to supervise lessons. We sat at picnic tables and worked at sheets of paper with schoolwork tasks appropriate for our age levels. I did simple arithmetic problems that day. But it certainly wasn't like being in a real school, learning something new!

June came and the Winslows delayed their trek east to the Thousand Islands because Uncle Max and Aunt Millie had come west and rented a home in Beverly Hills. When school was out, Aunt Millie invited Mommie Winslow and me to come and spend an afternoon enjoying the swimming pool in the back yard. It was the first private swimming pool I had ever seen or used. Mommie Winslow came fully dressed with her large hat and sun glasses and sat poolside listening to a portable radio which informed us of the "Fall of France" to Hitler's advancing troops. Aunt Millie and I swam, but I could overhear the conversation between the two women, both of whom had been to Paris and loved it. I would later understand the poignancy of the song, "The Last Time I Saw Paris," encapsulating grief over the darkness that had descended on "The City of Light." Tired, late afternoon, I was sent home in the Gordons' chauffeur-driven maroon Lincoln Zephyr. Like the Winslows, neither of the couple drove an automobile, and so needed a driver in a city that was so spread out as was Los Angeles.

We moved again at the end of June, and this time, only a few blocks south, to 1260 N. Laurel Avenue. The house was smaller than our previous ones, the rooms not as large, a typical 1920s style California bungalow. Grandmother was still living with us, and the boys needed a room, as well as my parents, so the breakfast room, so often a part of these older bungalows, became my bedroom. Somehow Dad managed to get my three-piece bedroom set in the confines of that small breakfast room, but there was no space left over in which to play. So I played outdoors in the tree-shaded yard.

There was a huge avocado tree next to the garage and I played there, often staring at, but standing apart from, the glass cages in which my middle brother kept his collection of snakes. Roger roamed the Hollywood Hills gathering them, once obtaining even a young rattlesnake, which my Mother promptly made him take back to the hills.

There was also a little trellis and gate between our property and that of our neighbors', an elderly couple. A niece of theirs, named Frances, visited them from Washington State. She was sixteen years old, very pretty, and she wanted to go to the beach every day. Fearing she might get "into trouble," all by herself, her uncle asked my parents if I might accompany her to the beach on a daily basis. Permission was granted. I had one of the most joyful summers a child of nine could ever wish for!

Frances and I would leave midmornings and be driven out Sunset Boulevard to where that road meets the sea. Her aunt always packed us a lunch. I built all kinds of things in the wet sand and splashed around in the shallow waves. After lunch, I lay on a towel in the warm sun and had a nap, listening to the gentle lapping of waves on the shore. Who knows what Frances did during this daily interlude? I know she talked to boys she met at the beach, but if she ever went off with them while I was asleep, I never knew. Then it would be late afternoon and her uncle called for us again. I was sad when summer ended and Frances went back to finish her high school.

The Laurel Avenue neighborhood, set between Sunset Boulevard on the north, and Santa Monica Boulevard on the south, was a typical middle-class Hollywood neighborhood for that time. It was full of people who worked for or at the movie studios or those who were considered artists. For instance, two old screen actresses lived with their many cats just south of our house. Further down the street was screen-writer, Forrest Barnes, who specialized in penning historical "shorts," and had won the 1936 Academy Award for a short about Patrick Henry. He lived with his novelist wife, Evelyn, and their newly adopted son, Christopher, a year or so younger than I. Directly across the street was James Swinnerton, famed western artist and cartoonist for the *Canyon Kiddies*. In the next block north, lived the in-laws of actor Ray Milland. The writer F. Scott Fitzgerald, who did some screen writing of his own, died that fall of 1940 from a heart attack in a Laurel Avenue apartment. Until his death, my brother Paul had sold him his evening paper.

But ours was not an uncommon Hollywood neighborhood. My good friend Phyllis Lundine, living a few streets east of us, could boast that her mother cooked for many movie stars, particularly on "the cook's day off (Thursday)." Astrid Lundine was a superb cook. I loved being invited for dinner or an overnight at the Lundine home, for not only did I relish her delicious meals, but also I could ask her about the show business people she fed. Her own favorites were Jack Benny and Mary Livingston, and she particularly liked the night Ingrid Bergman had come to dinner at the Benny home. This beautiful actress, fairly new to Hollywood then, came with her physician husband. When the meal was finished, before Astrid could clear the table, Bergman carried the dishes from the dining room to the kitchen, just for the fun of talking Swedish to Sweden-born Astrid. The actress' somber husband had to come out to the kitchen to retrieve her to join the others in the dining room.

Every child is blessed who has a teacher that inspires the child to learn about the world we share. That teacher for me was Hardinia Franklin, a middle-aged, plain-looking spinster, daughter of a well-to-do "old Los Angeles" family. She had traveled to all parts of the world, sharing her experience of having been bombed in Shanghai by the Japanese, and visiting the Parthenon and Acropolis in Greece. Through her, the map I carried in my head now incorporated the whole globe with its various continents.

Miss Franklin saw something in me that needed to "get out," needed to be expressed or externalized. The class was polishing shells she had gathered from the seashore and I spilled the bottle of oil we used for the polishing. She yelled at me in surprise, but after class that day, apologized for her outburst, and took me upon her lap. "What does your father do?" she asked. Perhaps she thought he could afford to replace the expensive polishing oil.

"He's a janitor," I answered. He had gotten a job as a night janitor for the Famous Department Store in Pasadena, and would drive the first of

Los Angeles' freeways to get there each night. From then on, Miss Franklin gave me special tasks to do for her, — take messages to the office, read announcements over the loud-speaker for morning assembly, — and so forth. School, and pleasing her, and learning all she was teaching, became the joy of my life. My world had expanded rapidly beyond the triangle of the three homes of which I was a part!

One day when Jack called for me at school and took me out to the Hillcrest to pick up Daddy Max after golf and a game of cards, Daddy Max said, "I want you to meet someone." He checked out the locker room to make sure no one was in a state of undress, then took me to a bench where Mickey Rooney, young, and at the height of his new popularity, was tying his shoes. "Mick," said Daddy Max, "This is my little girl, and I wanted you to meet her. Laura June, this is Mickey Rooney." There were pre-pubescent stirrings and stars in my eyes for days and weeks afterwards!

Another night, the Winslows joined the Reingolds for dinner at Chasen's, not our usual site to have dinner. I learned the reason later. Uncle Moe had opened a posh new jewelry store on a Beverly Hills corner intersecting Wilshire Boulevard. The store had his last name in big gold letters facing the corner. He was to meet someone at the store after-hours, so this person could make a purchase without a crowd recognizing her or noting what she bought. We were invited into the store when Uncle Moe opened it and turned on the lights. Alice Faye arrived shortly afterwards. She was so beautiful, and so sweet. She noticed me staring at her in awe, and after introductions, she took my hand and together we walked from one jewelry case to another eyeing their contents. "Do you like that, Laura June?" she would ask. "Don't you think this emerald is the prettiest?" I nodded yes, but too soon it was time for the Winslows to take me back to my home in Hollywood. It was a school-night.

About this time, my Great-Uncle Horace Kibbee, Grandmother's brother, retired from years as a printer in Eureka, California. Social welfare for the elderly had just come into being. "Unkie," as my sister Joyce called him, proposed that he and Grandmother pool their newly found social benefits, and together rent a cottage somewhere nearby. Grandmother moved out of our household, and the Williams family now numbered only seven.

Grandmother Reese and 'Unkie' Horace, her brother.

I never once left from an evening or day with the Winslows that Daddy Max did not open his wallet and remove a five, ten or twenty dollar bill, shove it into my pocket, and say to me, "Honey, when you get home, you give this to your Mother or Dad." And I always did, and it really helped our family get through the long dragged-out economic Depression. Dad was earning but a hundred dollars a month to look after a family of eight, until Grandmother moved on. Once that year, my baby sister, then a toddler, appeared in *One Million, B.C.*, a fanciful Hal Roach production about prehistoric times. It starred Victor Mature, Carole Landis and Lon Chaney, Jr. The pay, for whatever movie "extra work" that any of us landed, surely augmented the family income.

Besides the abiding generosity of Daddy Max toward our family, I was witness to Mommie Winslow's compassionate concern for a whole host of people. Many of the Tuesdays and Thursdays that Jack picked me up at school would be devoted to accompanying Mommie Winslow in visiting people who were ill or down and out, mostly former vaudevillians, musicians, actors or singers. Together we knocked at the doors of dumpy little rooms and apartments all over Hollywood. I didn't know the former celebrities we would be visiting, but Mommie Winslow made it clear to me that folks, who had once made others laugh or sing, deserved dignity when they fell upon hard times and were forgotten by the crowds they had entertained. Her gracious presence, plus a tin of cookies, or a small bouquet of flowers, or an envelope with money in it, — all these brightened many a face that had once, but no longer, looked out upon theater audiences.

The Christmas of 1940 the Winslows gave me a small radio for my bedroom. Radio drama was at its heights of achievement in those times, and so I treasured having it right next to my bed where I could listen to nightly dramas until nine o'clock, bedtime and "lights out." My favorite was the weekly production of *Henry Aldrich*.

Well into the fourth grade, my teacher, Miss Franklin, was teaching us to form paragraphs and think about topics we might write about in a paragraph or two. She may have suggested, "Write about your parents or your family." In any case, I wrote that I had three pairs of parents, and I remember calling them, "rich," "medium," and "poor." My mother was furious when I brought the composition home from school.

"You have only one set of parents, and don't you ever forget it!" she scowled, and spoke to me with that edge in her voice that I had come to dread. But I didn't re-write the paragraph, because in my nine-year-old mind and experience, it did seem that I had three sets of parents, that mine was a triangulated life.

I never had the pleasure of meeting Irving Berlin. Mr. Berlin and his wife and three young daughters preferred being in New York City three-quarters of the year, with only summers elsewhere, and the summer residence they chose was often a beach house at Santa Monica. But Jack and the Winslows would be away at the Thousand Islands simultaneously, so our paths were never to cross. However, once on a flying trip to Los Angeles, Berlin met with Daddy Max at the end of the trip. Max accompanied him to the airport. They must have been discussing their little girls, for just as the noted composer turned to bid his old friend goodbye, he drew from his luggage, a small ceramic Easter bunny, mounted atop a music-box that played his song, "Easter Parade." "Max, I was going to take this home for my daughters, but I want your little Laura June to have it. Here, give it to her, from me!" And Daddy Max put it in my hands when next I went to the Chateau.

1941 would be for me, as for the nation, a turning point year. Some years are like hinges on which a personal or national history turns in a totally new direction. School, and doing well academically, began to mean everything to me. I shared that with Mommie Winslow and she said that she and Daddy Max were thinking about sending me to college in a few years. I heard names like Bryn Mawr, Vassar, Smith, and Radcliffe. I had never traveled beyond California, but I began to imagine myself going east on the Super Chief when I was graduated from high school. That germ of a dream was planted that year.

In March, little Guy Kibbee Jr. experienced asthma breathing problems. His parents wanted my mother to serve as his governess and take my sister and him to that area nestled up against the mountains where the city air was cleaner and clearer. Mother agreed, and Aunt Brownie rented a cottage for the three of them in La Crescenta. Who would take care of me, on a daily basis, with Dad working nights and daytimes too, doing "odd jobs?" Chester was holding down at least two or three jobs, while Paul and Roger were still in school. Mama Lee and Daddy Carl came to the rescue, and said I could come and stay with them on Gage Avenue until school was out. I transferred to Budlong Avenue School where I had another inspiring teacher, only younger than Miss Franklin. We had lots of field trips to museums and the La Brea Tar Pits.

When Daddy Carl had returned from the cross-country tour of the South in fall 1939, he took employment with Donald Douglas Aircraft, sometimes working at the Santa Monica plant and sometimes at the firm's El Segundo location. In the quiet, behind-the-scenes mobilization for wartime production that was occurring, Carl was beginning to be recognized for his great engineering and problem-solving skills.

I renewed friendships from when I was little, and met a new little friend, just out from Ohio, Barbara Ann Hummel. But still my very best friend was Roslyn. Her mother and father had a son, and like my baby brother who had died, he had been named Richard. Now I spent overnight visits at her home. But the next year her handsome young father, Murray, would die from a sudden heart attack. In these present days of advanced medical care, it is hard to realize how many children were left orphaned in the 1930s and 1940s, but it was not an uncommon event.

I missed seeing Mommie Winslow and Daddy Max on a regular basis, but we talked on the phone, and once during the three months I was at the Ingrams', Jack drove her down to have afternoon tea with us. Come June, they would leave for what would be their last summer at the Thousand Islands. There was another ending in the life of Aunt Rose Cohn, when at last she went to Reno in July of 1941, and granted Uncle Harry the divorce he had wanted for years. She moved out of the Fremont Place home and into the Hotel Royale, closer to Hollywood on Rossmore Avenue.

1941 was full of firsts and lasts for me, —the first time I played miniature golf, the first time I saw a present-day supermarket, with its metal shopping carts, the first time I saw milk sold in square cartons instead of glass bottles. The times, they were a'changin'! President Roosevelt was beginning his third term in the Presidency, the first President to be elected to a third term. And it was the first time I ever saw a live person wear a strapless evening dress. I was at Mommie Winslow's for dinner and the Max Gordons were in town and staying at the Chateau. They stopped by to say hello to me on their way out to a gala event. Uncle Max had on his tuxedo, and Aunt Millie slipped off her fur coat to reveal a sequined strapless gown. She was exquisitely beautiful! It would be the last time I would see her for twelve years.

Movie stars often came to play tennis at the Chateau's tennis court. Big Bill Tilden, then retired from tennis competitions, was the hotel's "pro," designated to teach tennis. One afternoon, beautiful, soft-spoken Olivia de Haviland, was on the court for her lesson. It was not going too well. She swore like a sailor. I was aghast! I couldn't believe it! The bubble of illusion burst! Childhood, with its innocence, was ending. Something new and different was beginning. A ten-year-old catches the first glimpse that, from now on, life will be full of good-byes as well as helloes. Nothing lasts forever, and everything changes!

Laura June Kenny

Mommie Winslow and Daddy Max, their last summer in the Thousand
Islands.

CHAPTER 3

HELLOES AND GOODBYES: THE WORLD WAR II YEARS AND AFTER
1941-46

Change was in the air that summer of 1941! At age twenty-six, Jack Calhoun received one of the first draft notices prior to World War II. He left the employ of the Winslows, as their driver, to take up basic training for the Army, but only after delivering to them their new car, a black 1942 Dodge. Jack was assigned first to Fort Ord, then sent to bivouac, camped just outside the Ahwahnee Hotel in Yosemite, where three years before, he and I had spent a week, along with Mommie Winslow. When the Winslows returned from what turned out to be their last summer in the Thousand Islands, they had to hire a new driver. I had difficulty getting used to the new chauffeur. He certainly was not like another big brother to me!

The adjustment in circumstances proved hard for Mommie Winslow, as well. Jack had not only been her driver for five years, but a pal, a confidante, almost the son she had never borne. Some time before that summer she had set up a Ping-Pong table in the middle of her large antique-furnished living room. I loved to watch Mommie Winslow and Jack play a game or two in late afternoons, before he went to pick up Daddy Max at his office or the

Hillcrest Club. It was all in good fun, and there was lots of laughter, as the duo sought to avoid hitting either a priceless Meissen lamp or a pair of sandwich glass candy dishes that were displayed on a what-not stand.

Then too, Jack, as a twenty plus young man, kept up with all that was "new," what today would be called "trendy." Tillie had loved being taken by him into the world of young people and their interests: the new restaurants called "drive-ins," where waitresses skated to the side of your car to take your order, and the new spectator sport called "the roller derby." Jack even introduced her to the budding celebrities of the sport, and brought them to the Chateau for a visit. (At its inception, the participants of the roller derby were rather gentle people, very athletic, but not as fiercely competitive as they later became.) Now, with Jack gone, all the Winslows had was an efficient driver, who is nameless and faceless in my memory!

Change marked the life of Mama Lee and Daddy Carl as well. Carl had been employed at Douglas Aircraft for two years now, developing the initial tool-and-dye design for the landing gear of that great aircraft workhorse of the war that was coming, the magnificent DC-3. Douglas wanted him to transfer to its new Long Beach plant.

Carl's aged parents and one brother lived in El Monte, so the Ingrams began house hunting there and found a luxury home among the dense walnut groves of southeast El Monte. The September of 1941, the Ingrams left their first home, the Gage Avenue residence they had built shortly after their marriage in 1929. My weekend visits were scheduled less often than before, because of the greater driving distance from El Monte to Hollywood, and I missed the familiar bungalow to which I had been brought, as a toddler, nine years before.

However, the new home sat on a half-acre, had extensive flower and vegetable gardens and fruit trees, and Lee and Carl could even raise chickens and ducks. When I visited there, I liked waking up listening to roosters crowing in the early mornings. In the late afternoons, it was not unusual to hear hungry lions roar for their afternoon hunk of horse meat at Gay's Lion Farm, about a mile and a half distant. Leo, the M-G-M. insignia lion, was housed there, as were other show business big cats. And I could walk just half a block to get freshly bottled milk from a neighborhood dairy. The extended clan of the Ingrams gathered often, either at Lee's and Carl's, or the nearby home of his parents. I enjoyed the company of my many Ingram "cousins" at these weekend gatherings.

And I was changing too, for sure! The year I was eight, my long curls had been cut and I had been given a smelly permanent, sitting beneath a contraption with many wires that looked like it belonged in a medieval torture chamber. At school, I dropped the name of Laura and wanted to be known as "June," instead. Ever since I had been in Miss Franklin's fourth grade class, boys in the class teased me and asked, "What are those bumps in the front of your dress?" Obviously, I was early in developing breasts, and by the time I was ten and in fifth grade, Mother had to take me to the J.C. Penney store on Hollywood Boulevard and buy me a "starter brassiere." In fact, that piece of clothing was the first she had purchased for me except for my baby clothes, just over a decade before.

Through the years, many have asked me why I stopped appearing in films, let alone my disappearance from the *Little Rascals* movies. Physical growth and change become the major and simple answer to that query! Contrary to popular belief, the bodies of children do not grow consistently and uniformly, but rather in spurts. In teacher training I was to learn that at age five, the legs of little ones, particularly their thigh bones or femurs, lengthen markedly. Then at age six, the torso catches up. And so it is in late childhood, ages eight, nine, ten and eleven, there are obvious spurts and plateaus in children's physical growth, a certain unevenness in growth and development.

Truly the beginning of "The Curse of the Little Rascals" is that they don't stay little any more! There is a gangling, awkward stage around ages nine, ten and eleven, when children those ages cannot possibly look like the "cuties" they were at five, six, seven, or even eight years. No amount of costuming will hide a child's movement into pre-pubescence.

Take a look at "Alfalfa" in the Rascals' *Practical Jokers*, released December 1938 when he was eleven. He has begun to tower over "Spanky," "Porky" and "Buckwheat." His facial features begin to show harbingers of how he will look in his adolescence in scenes from *Cousin Wilbur*, released just four months later. He would leave the Rascals in November 1940, having just entered his teenage years.

Then consider Darla, just my age, when she begins stretching out into her late childhood form. The viewer will notice that from 1940 on, she is dressed with straps of overalls and jumpers to cover her budding womanhood. In December 1941, at age ten, Darla will be seen for the last time in the Rascals' short, *Wedding Worries*.

Unexpected Riches, released October 1942 marks George "Spanky" McFarland's last appearance in the *Our Gang Comedies*, and not a year too soon, as he was already a teenager, trying to pass as a boy in late childhood. Dressing him up in short pants didn't help! "Buckwheat" Billie Thomas perseveres to the last episode of the last *Little Rascals* film, *Tale of a Dog*, released in April 1944, but again, short pants fail to hide his pubescent spurt.

M-G-M studios permanently shut down the *Little Rascals* film production in 1944. For many of the former Rascals, this closure marked "the end of the line," finis, to a show business career. They were more or less discarded as child performers, left to search for hard-to-find employment in the entertainment business. Or, if they were lucky, like "Spanky" McFarland, they had a parent who wisely removed them from the Hollywood scene. His father took him back to Texas, and I once heard him say it was fun, "just to go fishing," and experience something of a normal adolescence.

Of course, the real reason I escaped "The Curse of the Little Rascals," was because, at some level, I had chosen to escape, that long ago day of the screen test, knowing, from deep down inside my five-year-old head, that I didn't want what being in the movies meant. For me, it would have meant Mother's total control of my life, so that those two other sets of nurturing foster parents would have been ushered out, and shut out of my life. Besides, I could never forget the early risings, the long ten-hour days at the studios five days a week, the resultant fatigue, and the loss of any semblance of normal family life.

Even as a pre-teen, there were no rewards I could see for "being in the movies," but instead, plenty of losses, though I could not verbalize them then. Viewing child stardom as a very mature adult now, and especially from the perspective of having been a teacher for thirty-six years, the losses *far* outweigh the rewards for children in show business.

Had I, as a child, gained a certain movie stardom, what could I have listed as the expected rewards? That's easy: fame, fortune, celebrity and glamour. Wow, you might think, — every child's fairy-tale dream come true! Who wouldn't go for that? Better we flip these coins of the realm called, "The rich and famous," and examine their tarnished, corrosive undersides, *the predominant losses that most child movie stars or performers suffer.* The authentic "Curse of the Little Rascals" is the accumulated combination of these ongoing losses, whereas most people think of the "Curse" only in terms of the sad and sorry endings to the histories of so many former members of *Our Gang Comedies.*

The first of these losses is *the loss of childhood.* It is an obvious given of nature that each human being born is granted only *a one-time opportunity to be a child.* I once heard Elizabeth Taylor, speaking on the *Larry King Live* television show, discuss her own "loss of childhood" that she experienced as a very young actress. During the same broadcast, she also mentioned a similar fate for her friend Michael Jackson in his show business career. Then the more recent allegations with regard to Michael Jackson brought forth a TV interview in which a psychologist posited that the "King of Pop" might have suffered since childhood, from what the psychologist termed "*a deficit in peer group*" syndrome.

No amount of money earned, filling the hours, providing entertainment for the public, can ever compensate for the absence of all the learnings for which the experience of childhood provides spacious time and space. Among all the species of mammals, only the slow maturation of *homo sapiens*, —us, — allows for a span of nearly two decades in which to grow and develop. During this long interval, we human beings begin to make and to configure all the associations and neural connections that need to be made using our bigger brains. We call this long span childhood and adolescence. A "childhood lost," no matter what amount of wealth is accumulated in the process, is indeed a "Paradise lost!"

What about the fame and celebrity that come the way of young entertainers? Don't they constitute gains rather than losses? Yes, if you want a good table at a gourmet restaurant, or prime seats for some event, yes, they do! But balance these perks off with *the loss of privacy*, and the mark one becomes for being stalked, or written up or photographed for the tabloids. Remember young Rebecca Schaeffer, a model at age sixteen, then a television star in *My Sister Sam* before she was twenty? She was shot in 1989 by a crazed fan who had stalked her!

Recently I attended a writers' conference in Hollywood where a very beautiful but no longer active movie star was a presenter of awards. It saddened me to see her accompanied and surrounded at all times by four bodyguards. And yet she was among a crowd of admirers, well-wishers and very refined people, not a crowd of gawking, clawing fans on a sidewalk! I contrast this to the Hollywood scene in which I grew up, where you could buy your toothpaste at a drugstore and be standing in line next to a familiar face like Dane Clark's or Van Hefflin's. I learned early on that movie stars were really "ordinary people," with ordinary needs and wants. They bought their afternoon newspapers from newsboys like my brother Paul who sold them on the corner of Sunset and Laurel Canyon Boulevards. They even had to purchase toilet paper just like the rest of us mortals! But set apart, as "special people," movie stars are made to lose "the common touch," their ordinariness as human beings, and when it occurs in childhood, that's a terrible *loss of self-perspective.*

The long childhood afforded human beings, if not interrupted by the need to be employed as a performer, allows for individuation and establishment of the self. That wonderful educator, Maria Montessori, described "play" as the real work of children. Growing up naturally, not having to play set roles, makes for a gradual separation of the self from adults and peers as the young child begins to define himself or herself, to achieve that unique identity that each individual possesses. And this happens most often through what we call "child's play," also called "dramatic play," by kindergarten teachers like myself. This can happen beautifully if you, as a child, are allowed to grow to be the person you were meant to be. Suppose, however, you are asked or forced "to be" or to portray someone else, even a child similar to yourself. When and where do you find your own *authentic selfhood* if you are asked to think and act like another, say, eight hours a day, five days a week, many dozens of weeks a year?

One of the greatest losses suffered by child performers is that *their childhood is used as a means to better others, mostly adults, and mostly financially, but sometimes even psychologically.* Since children began appearing in show business, they have been used as the tools to gain financial success for adults. Doesn't society now normally frown on child labor?

Jackie Coogan earned two million dollars appearing in films in the 1920's. His mother and stepfather siphoned off and spent most of his earnings. When he finally took them to court in 1938 and sued them for the money he had earned, he was awarded one-half of all that was left, $125,000.00! The California legislature then enacted *The Child Actors Law* in 1939, often referred to as the *Coogan Law*. This law designates that earnings be placed in a trust, a fund held until the child reaches his or her majority. Even with this law, the intent has since been subverted by the hiring of a retinue of people, supposedly to serve the needs of the child performer, persons such as managers, accountants, lawyers, public relations personnel, etc. I have heard former child star, Gary Coleman, describe how he and his earnings went their separate ways by the employment of just such an entourage of hangers-on!

Worse than the subtle theft and the fraud often perpetrated, in this manner, is what happens to a child performer when she or he looks around and sees so many others dependent upon how he or she performs for the camera or for an audience. It's called *the rapid discovery of exploitation!*

In my thirty-six years of teaching, I regularly had children perform in skits or small plays. They loved the experience, as did their parents and friends who watched. But these small dramatic presentations were only the *vehicles* for all kinds of other, more significant learnings, such as working cooperatively with others, building self-esteem, paying attention and communicating more freely. Exposure to reading, history, art and music also made the scene. *The play was not the thing*! *Learning was*!

To be used psychologically by an adult to promote the emotional well-being of that adult is perhaps the worst of fates that befall a young entertainer. We are all familiar with the image of the "stage mother," the mother who hovers over her youngster making sure he or she gets the best part or the most perks. *That hovering individual is seeking her own identity by promoting the superficial, but not the authentic, identity of a child. That's called projection*! Father figures can also be found guilty of this subtle form of child abuse! Consider Macauley Culkin, star of the *Home Alone* movie, who took a hiatus in his career, as a teen-ager, to get himself out from under what he considered parental domination. No child should be asked to be responsible for the emotional equilibrium or sense of fulfillment of any adult.

Finally, child performers almost routinely lose *a basic sense of values*, values like building relationships versus the acquisition of material things. To be able to buy whatever one fancies, for oneself or even to give to others, is to open a Pandora's box of troubles. For when the tough times come, and they do, to all of us, young or old, no matter what our bank account says, *what really matters is whom we love, who loves us, and how we may have helped to make our world a better place, how we made a difference for good*. When these wonderful, old-fashioned values take a backseat to buying and selling, then poor life-choices are made, and young celebrities often resort to drugs, alcohol, and sex as the means to fill that empty space where real human values should have been ingrained in their psyches.

The histories of young Todd Bridges and Dana Plato, stars of the sit-com *Diff'rent Strokes*, illustrate, all too well, the downward spiral caused by a loss of values. To his credit, Todd Bridges has been sober and productive as an actor for the last few years but he lost a decade of his young manhood pursuing the drug scene. Tragically, Dana Plato ended her life in a drug suicide, after having been twice arrested in the early 1990s.

I remember long ago reading a book by Diana Barrymore titled, *Too Much, Too Soon*. Barrymore was the aunt of Drew Barrymore and daughter of eminent actor John Barrymore, who appeared on both stage and in sixty-five films before his death in 1942. She grew up with plenty of wealth and exposure to the world of stage and screen, but with little love from her parents. No values at all, nor purpose to her life, it seemed. At one time she herself had a promising career in movies and in the legitimate theater. But she chose abusive husbands and deadened her inner turmoil with alcohol. She died at age thirty-eight. The title of her book says it all! Without the grounding of deep values and being loved, but possessing "too much" of material goods, one can leave this world much "too soon." Sadly, that fate befell too many former "Little Rascals!"

Blessedly, as a child, I did not have to endure these losses I've enumerated, but there were other losses on the horizon in that fall of 1941. The Winslows were hardly back in town from their summer sojourn when October 8 brought the news of the sudden death of their close friend, my Uncle Gus Kahn, the lyricist of the title song of *One Night of Love*, the film Daddy Max had brought into being back in 1934. I had just come home from school and found Dad, as usual, listening to one of the many afternoon newscasts on the radio. The announcer declared, "Today Hollywood lost one of its finest composers of movie music, Gus Kahn. Kahn died from a heart attack in his Beverly Hills home." Dad was fixing supper, but I wandered out into the yard to mull over this sad news. My friend Roslyn had lost her father Murray from a sudden heart attack the previous May, and she was only ten, like me. Death became a fact of life I knew I would encounter from that point on!

Two weeks and two days later, Victor Schertzinger, the kindly composer and director who had spent an afternoon, six years before, making photographic portraits of me, also died. He had collaborated with Uncle Gus, composing the music to accompany the lyrics of the title song. As well, Schertzinger had directed the film. Both men had illustrious and prolific careers, Gus dying at age fifty-five, and Victor at fifty-one. We still hear the music each created, decades after their deaths. That tried and true standard, "It Had To Be You," is the foremost musical legacy left by Uncle Gus. The song, "Tangerine," and "I Remember You," were Schertzinger's. Makes one think the old adage is true, "Music alone shall live!"

In November, Daddy Max and Mommie Winslow were invited to the Kahns for Thanksgiving. Mommie Winslow told me afterwards, "Laura June, it was beautiful to see how Uncle Gus's son Donald took his place at the head of the table and carved the turkey for all of us. It was sad, too, for we missed Gus, but Donald took charge, just like Gus would have wanted him to." Mommie Winslow was forever gently pointing to human behavior she found admirable, wise or courageous, thus mentoring me as well as mothering me! Hers was a different way of being, and I loved her for that!

And in the months to follow, Mommie Winslow marveled at how Aunt Grace took hold of the couple's business affairs with a firm and steady hand. "Laura June, when you grow up, learn as much as you can about your husband's business affairs, so you can step right in to take care of all the things you have to do after your husband dies. Aunt Grace is terrific at this!"

Then it was the first week of December and the golden bells and red ribbons were hung on the front door of the Winslows' apartment. The two card tables were put in place, and their living room became the center for wrapping presents and writing cards. While Mommie Winslow made magic emerge from tissue paper and ribbons, I sat looking over the Christmas cards that had arrived. There was a picture card from Grace Moore and her husband Val, greetings from the Irving Berlins and the Max Gordons, and even one from Sophie Tucker and another from Jimmy Durante. Jack drove me home from the Chateau, not his fast, back street route, but along Hollywood Boulevard so that I could see the lampposts decked out as huge lighted Christmas trees. The nightly parade with Santa Claus on his float, a movie star at his side, had already passed, so we were free to pass the length of the boulevard from Vine Street to La Brea Avenue and enjoy the annual beauty.

Sunday morning, December 7, I had just come home from Sunday School, changed into play clothes and was outside at the trellis that marked the gate between our neighbors and ourselves. It had a little bench where I could sit. Mother came out on the side-porch of our house, calling to me, "June, it's war! Come inside and listen to the radio. The Japanese have just bombed Pearl Harbor, in Hawaii." I don't remember the rest of the day, but events of the next morning are clear in memory.

I went to school on Monday morning, and immediately all classes went to the school auditorium. Our fifth grade class was one of the last to enter and there was no place else for us to sit except on the floor in front of the stage where a large radio had been placed. The Principal told us to sit very quietly as President Roosevelt was going to address the Congress and speak by radio to the whole country as well. During the course of his speech, in which he said those famous words about December 7 being, "A day that will live in infamy," he also made reference to the Members of Congress just in front of him. Part of his statement made reference to "Those of you on the floor," at which remark some of my class giggled and tittered because we thought he was speaking about us, and how did he know where we were sitting?

Christmas was subdued that year. The Winslows gave me clothes, candies and children's books about opera and classical composers. Their big gift was a series of War Bonds, all wrapped in a package of red, white and blue. Those bonds would see me through a semester at U.C.L.A. ten years later! People didn't know what to expect. Would the Japanese attempt to shell or bomb mainland California? Civil defense units were formed very quickly and neighborhoods were told to buy blinds to shield the windows of homes during the black-outs that were expected.

There had been turbulence in our household as well. My middle brother Roger was in high school and he was very bright, so brilliant he often failed to do the required homework because he knew, when he went to class, he could produce whatever answers were required on the spot. This became a source of friction between him and our Mother. There were other issues, but I didn't know of them. I only knew, when he graduated Hollywood High at the end of January, a month before he turned eighteen, he moved out of our house and up the street to a neighbor's garage room, which he rented. He got a job at Lederle Laboratories and slept and ate in that small room. I hated it that he had to eat alone, food which he heated over a Sterno can. I went to see him often, as the widow who rented him the room, had a daughter I could play with before he arrived home from work.

I learned that winter, when I was in fifth grade, something of the humanness of my schoolteacher, Edith E. Stewart. I had been absent with a bad cold and she phoned my home one afternoon asking that I call her back in the evening to get the reading assignment. When I reached her apartment by phone, she answered, but promptly excused herself for a minute "to turn a steak" on her stove. "Teachers eat steak, how amazing!" I thought, but I shouldn't have been surprised because, before that, she had told me she had seen the film "Rebecca" at the Pantages Theater. And I had been amazed then that teachers, whom I had put high upon a pedestal, even went to see movies!

In 1942, my brother Paul appeared momentarily as an extra in "Miss Annie Rooney," the film in which teenager Shirley Temple received her first kiss from former *Little Rascal*, Dickie Moore. Paul was seen but a moment, but oh, how handsome he was, fifteen going on sixteen, decked out in a tuxedo. I hadn't liked seeing myself in movies, but I was really thrilled to see my brothers whenever I caught glimpses of them in films. Uncle Guy Kibbee was also part of the cast, playing Grandpa Rooney.

Before the advent and widespread use of penicillin, illness hit my family big-time in March of 1942. My Dad and my two brothers, Paul and Chester, and even my little sister Joyce all became ill with pneumonia. Mother asked Lee and Carl to take me to their home again and enroll me in the nearest school, just as they had done the previous spring. I finished grade five at Mountain View School in El Monte, and for the first time rode a bus to school rather than walking.

Mama Lee was making many new friends in El Monte, and among them were musicians who needed a pianist for a small dance band that played for local dances. Daddy Carl, a wonderful dancer, taught me to dance that spring on many a Friday and Saturday night. He was six feet tall, and I barely stood tall enough to reach where his tie ended, but I loved moving to music, and the tunes of the early 1940s were so danceable. Among them was Victor Schertzinger's "Tangerine," becoming a big hit after his death.

Daddy Max became ill that spring also. For many years I thought penicillin might have spared his death, had it been available in early 1942. But within this last decade Jack was to tell me he was certain Daddy Max did not die from pneumonia, as his death certificate stated, or if he did, pneumonia was not the primary cause of death. Jack was certain Max Winslow died from undiagnosed lung cancer. He had smoked for many years. In the spring of 1942, Jack had returned to Hollywood, after having been given a compassionate discharge from the Army, to ease the burden for his own family when his mother suffered a stroke. His being in town allowed him also to be like a son to the ailing Max Winslow. He came almost every day and gave Max back rubs. When Max felt up to it, Jack drove him out to Beverly Hills, to a grassy space on Benedict Canyon Road where he could shoot a few golf balls around. He was no longer able to visit his beloved Hillcrest Country Club for golf and cards.

I never got to say "good-bye" to Daddy Max. My living in El Monte, thirty-five miles distant from Hollywood, and gas rationing just having been instituted, was the primary reason, though not the whole reason. Mommie Winslow was relying on Christian Science to heal his condition and restore him to health. Purely from love, she didn't want me to see him so ill and deteriorating. On my eleventh birthday, June 8, 1942, she called to tell me Daddy Max had "passed on."

Not since the death of my brother Richard, six and a half years before, had I confronted such a palpable sense of grief and loss. Dickie's death had certainly cast a long shadow of sorrow over our family, but personally it had not left me bereft, for I hardly knew Dickie before he died. After all, I had lived with Mama Lee and Daddy Carl since before and after Dickie's birth in 1934. Now someone who had played such a huge part in my life was forever gone, and I would never see that person again. I did not attend the funeral of Daddy Max, and maybe it would have been better had I been allowed to participate in that ritual, as a way to deal with and work through my pre-teen unspoken grief.

Daddy Max, as I remember him, prior to his death.

Shirley Kibbee's eleventh birthday, ten days after mine, was to be celebrated at a party high atop Mount Wilson, with its observatory and picnic grounds. Aunt Brownie drove to El Monte to pick me up and I joined a carload of Shirley's friends from Beverly Hills. We toured the observatory grounds and had our picnic lunch, then took a walk on a mountain trail. For whatever reason, I lagged behind, stepped on slippery gravel and began to fall down a very steep slope. I grabbed a little bush on the way downhill and clung to it, yelling for help. To my rescue came young soldiers, part of an anti-aircraft artillery squadron stationed on that high mountain that overlooks the San Gabriel Valley. The soldiers formed a human chain, reaching down to me and securing me so I would fall no further. Then they drew me up the mountainside, hand over hand, and I was delivered to a very relieved Aunt Brownie. Looking back, I realize I must have been despondent over Daddy Max's death and "acted out" my despair by accidentally, on purpose, falling down that mountainside. It was a kind of "cry for help" from an eleven-year-old broken heart!

Mama Lee began to have her problems with me also, and sent me off to stay at Gram's cabin for the month of July. Somehow, the gentle pace of life with Gram served to heal my unspoken sorrow. The Williams family, minus my two older brothers who were in the process of preparing for basic training for the army, moved again, this time to the San Fernando Valley. Mother and Dad rented an empty farmhouse on a working farm, 6161 Whitsett Avenue, in North Hollywood. I returned to that residence about the first of August. Mother enlisted me to grind apricots while she cooked apricot marmalade. It was the first time we had worked in the kitchen side by side, in the six years since I had lived at home.

Tillie Winslow's oldest sister, Aunt Sally du Mond, died in mid-August. Mother and I went to her funeral at the Wee Kirk O' the Heather in Forest Lawn. When this death occurred, Mommie Winslow wanted me to see Aunt Sally laid out in the coffin. "She looks very beautiful, Laura June, and I don't want you to be afraid of seeing someone dead," she said as she took my hand. "You have to look death in the face, my dear, and not shrink from what it means," she added. I did go with her, after the funeral and before the burial, to see the woman who had literally raised Mommie Winslow after her own mother's death in childbirth. Two deaths in the space of ten weeks! I wondered how Mommie Winslow bore such sorrow.

I would learn in the months to follow, when I spent weekends with Mommie Winslow, that she let herself cry, and that it was all right to allow oneself time and space for grieving. She was not ashamed for me to see her weeping, nor did she stop me from crying when her tears brought my empathetic grief to the fore. Aunt Jane Winslow, Max's sister, who had lived with Aunt Sally for many years, now came to share the apartment at the Chateau with Mommie Winslow. Jane was a marvelous cook so "Room Service" was abandoned for good. Aunt Jane now slept in Daddy Max's bed and took his room for her own. The room remained furnished just the same, and seeing that sameness gave me comfort on my weekend visits.

Mommie Winslow gave Daddy Max's clothes to my father, who was about the same medium height and build. But one piece of his clothing remained hanging on the bathroom door, something Mommie Winslow could not bear to part with. For the rest of her life, she would gaze at Max's red silk robe, hung next to her "dressing gown." The sight of it comforted me also!

In our end-of-evening bedside chats that fall, Mommie Winslow spoke often of death, of the deaths of family members and friends. She told me how, when her sisters, Julia, and Theresa, had died, she was the only one who would sit "vigil" with them, as they were laid out, before burial, in the family parlor at Norwich, New York. "It didn't frighten me to sit there in the dark and the candlelight next to their coffins," she told me. Then she spoke of her brother Frank, a "minstrel man," in vaudeville, who had died from the effects of alcoholism some nine years before. Previously, we had visited his grave in Boyle Heights' Calvary Cemetery. On some of my weekend visits to the Chateau, Mommie Winslow would find someone to drive us to Forest Lawn to visit the graves of both Aunt Sally and Daddy Max. She had purchased a family plot in the Gardens of Memory, high atop a hill overlooking Los Angeles.

I attended Victory Boulevard School in September of 1942, and my teacher was Frieda K. McGuire. She had us reading the weekly *Scholastic* newspaper for schools. My interior map of the world again widened to now include the place names of all the fronts upon which the war was being waged in Southeast Asia, the Pacific Islands and North Africa. Deaths were not highlighted in the news, but each student in that class knew the difference between blue stars hanging in a small window flag versus their replacement with stars of gold! Sacrifice was asked for and observed by almost everyone. In the ensuing months and years, Aunt Jane Winslow's knitting needles were to produce hundreds of khaki sweaters for servicemen. Aunt Rose, never without a maid since she had married the lawyer Cromwell thirty years before, now scrubbed toilets and sinks in the Beverly Hills Canteen. Rationing of tires, coffee, butter, sugar and meat had been recently established. If a person went to dinner at a friend's, it was not unusual to make an offering of rationing stamps. Mother insisted upon this offering whenever I would spend an overnight at a girl friend's home.

Patriotism and sacrifice were themes being lived out in the lives of ordinary people. One day I penned a couple of paragraphs and left a copy of my effort on Mrs. McGuire's desk

An S. A. on Teachers

The American teacher is an American soldier, because her effort in this war is as strong as that of a Colonel or Ensign. Her effort is to teach children to make a better world for themselves when the war is over. And yet she receives no medals. But long ago she was given a wonderful medal—to have knowledge, truth, wisdom and courage. Children, as I am, have grown to love their teachers as a second mother.
I want to tell you to keep your eyes on the youth and watch them make their plans for a better world, this time for always. Keep your eye on the teacher too, the teacher who doesn't have a medal. Soon there will be one there. Her reward is just watching the children she taught to make a better world for a better people. Remember these four words—Future, Youth, Knowledge and Leadership, for they are the opening to a new and better and more peaceful world than we have now.

I had heard but not seen the names of various types of compositions, and concluded I would call my written offering an "S.A." My teacher later sent the above to be published in the magazine of the California Teachers Association, then called the *Sierra Educational News.*

At school, where I had recently been "skipped" a half grade, from the earlier half of grade six to its latter half, I was asked to sing, in the annual Christmas program, the role of one of the kings featured in the carol, "We Three Kings." I had little stage fright, for my brother Roger had been sending home money to my Mother, asking her to see to it I received singing lessons from his former vocal teacher, Jack Eastman. At eleven years, I felt totally competent to take a bus from school down to the old "Red Car," board it and move through the Cahuenga Pass, to Hollywood Boulevard and Highland Avenue. There I boarded another bus and went to the Sunset Strip area where Mr. Eastman had his studio. Sometimes, as well as the money from Roger, Mother had me take a dozen eggs to Mr. and Mrs. Eastman.

The eggs were ours to eat and give away, courtesy of actor Ray Milland, brother-in-law of brother Paul's best friend, Bobby Webber. "Jack," as my brothers called the movie star, had a flock of Bufforfington chickens he was no longer allowed to raise at his Beverly Hills estate, so our family became their keepers for a few months.

Christmas 1942 was as low-key as the previous Christmas had been, somber perhaps because two of my brothers were now in the service and away from home. Dad would soon be leaving to find "war work" in Northern California. There was no Balzer's delivery truck making its way to the Valley with boxes of food to be prepared for the Williams' Christmas feast. I spent much of the two-week Christmas holiday, dividing my time, with both Mommie Winslow and Aunt Jane in Hollywood, then with Mama Lee and Daddy Carl in El Monte. The Ingrams' dog Teddy had died that fall at the age of twelve, just falling asleep out in their sunny yard. He was not replaced, but someone gave Lee and Carl identical twin cats, and I enjoyed watching their antics on visits.

One day after Christmas, on my return trip from the Eastman residence and my voice lesson, I stopped to buy something at the corner drug store near the streetcar stop, on Hollywood Boulevard, where I was to take the "Red Car" back to the Valley. I missed my connection, and the next streetcar would be half an hour later. I called my Mother to confess my lagging behind schedule, and could tell from the tone of her voice she was furious about my tardiness. When I alighted from the car at the corner of Chandler and Whitsett Streets over an hour later, Mother was there to meet me and to walk me home in the near dusk of the evening. "That's it," she declared, "No more voice lessons for you. You can't be trusted to follow directions!" No amount of pleading on my part, nor promising to be more alert, prevailed. Any voice training thereafter took place only in a school setting.

In February I began seventh grade classes at North Hollywood Junior High, some distance from our home so bus transportation was provided. I felt very grown up. With Dad having gone to work in the shipyards at Stockton, Paul became "the man in the family," at age seventeen, and with a driver's license. But that status was short-lived, for in March, he dropped out of North Hollywood High School and joined the Merchant Marine. Since Mother did not drive, the car was sold and Mother moved Joyce and me out of the spacious farmhouse into a small cottage at the back of property owned by movie dog-trainer, Rudd Weatherwax. We never saw his famous canine movie star, "Lassie." However, living at 10915 Vanowen, we were witness to the daily trainloads of war equipment that rumbled not twenty feet from our back wall. The first night I slept in that house, I awoke screaming when the first steam locomotive made its way through the darkness. But it only took a few days before I could sleep through the noise and clatter of jeeps and tanks being moved on flat cars, throughout the night, to all the military bases up and down the state.

On one of the weekends I spent at Mommie Winslow's that spring, she announced she had a surprise for me. She had bought me a matinee ticket to see the Irving Berlin production, *This Is The Army*, which she, Aunt Jane and Aunt Rose had seen the week before. The next day, I would take the "Red Car" downtown to the Subway Terminal, then walk around the corner, the short distance to the Philharmonic Auditorium on the north side of Pershing Square. It was one of the first stage productions I had seen except when my brother Roger had appeared in a play in Hollywood. The cast and crew was huge, almost three hundred men, and the format was that of a musical revue. The highlight of the show was when Mr. Berlin, dressed in his World War I soldier's khaki uniform, sang his 1918 song, "Oh, How I Hate to Get Up in the Morning." The crowd roared with delight, and how I wished that Daddy Max were there to sit beside me and see what his "discovery" had wrought. That Berlin production, and its later movie adaptation, raised nearly ten million dollars for the Army Emergency Relief Fund.

When I returned to the Chateau at day's end, Mommie Winslow asked me to do the usual— to write a thank you letter to Mr. Berlin. I loved using the stationary provided by the hotel, with its engraved heading in fancy script, so that was no chore. And since Berlin was a great writer of thank you notes himself, I know he appreciated my eleven-year-old effort. I was just a few months older than his second daughter, Linda.

I was to learn sometime that year why Mommie Winslow always praised Aunt Grace Kahn's adeptness at business matters. One Saturday, when I was in Hollywood visiting with her, we were taken to lunch at the Beverly Hills Hotel by someone I had known as "Uncle Saul" Bornstein, a friend from New York and former fishing buddy of Daddy Max's. I did not know then that he had been the founding third partner in Irving Berlin, Inc. along with Berlin and Daddy Max. Mommie Winslow was insistent I accompany her to the luncheon, and now I realize I was there to act as a buffer, so Uncle Saul would not rage against Irving Berlin with whom he was in bitter dispute about the management of the firm. Mommie Winslow felt so inadequate to discuss business, to offer opinions or even to take sides, if that was what was required. It helped to have a child present to tone down the discussions that day! I sensed the tension in the air, and I never saw Mr. Bornstein after. Later Mommie Winslow would tell me he left the music publishing firm and formed his own in 1944, taking as his share of the company the musical rights to the *Pinocchio* and *Snow White* scores and other songs not written by Mr. Berlin himself.

What she did not tell me was that Mr. Bornstein got her to grant him something of monetary value, perhaps some of Daddy Max's shares in the firm, perhaps just her blessing as Winslow's widow. In exchange for her relinquishment, Tillie received from him land in Mississippi, later valued at $100,000, and I saw the land listed as containing turpentine pines. Mrs. Bornstein was also somehow involved in this land holding arrangement. No wonder Mommie Winslow felt so at a loss when making business decisions, and always urged me "to mind your husband's business affairs."

At school I took both cooking and sewing classes, "Home economics," the curricula notice named them. I loved the cooking class, but sewing was not "my cup of tea." The only sewing task I could accomplish well was the production of quilted mules for the servicemen who were beginning to return from battles, wounded and needing hospitalization. The Red Cross collected the dozens of flat house-slippers and invited those of us who could to accompany the slippers to their destination, Birmingham Military Hospital. One night a group of us girls were driven to the hospital and entered a recreation area where pajama-clad soldiers sat around in their bathrobes, playing cards and reading. Most of the men were no more than ten years older than we were. It was hard to make conversation with them, so we were relieved when the door opened and in came the evening's entertainment, no other than my Aunt Grace Kahn and a handsome young man named Desi Arnaz. This duo took turns playing the piano and singing requests from the soldier-patients.

I was so proud of Aunt Grace that night, and told her so when next we met. She asked me to stop by her house whenever I came to Beverly Hills to visit with my cousin Shirley Kibbee. Aunt Grace always had clothes to give me, either hers or those of her daughter Irene. On these occasions, she would take me into her sewing room, see where the outfit needed a tuck here or there, or some hemming, turn to her sewing machine and proceed to make the garment wearable for me, right then and there.

Since Mother was receiving some money from her soldier sons, "allotments," they called them, and also funds from Dad's higher wartime wages, she embarked upon a search to buy a house somewhere in the San Fernando Valley. Joyce and I were "in the way," so, of course, off we were sent to Mama Lee's for the summer. But Grandma Shaffer was now in her middle sixties and missing deeply the young man who had been like a son to her, Bill Jones. Bill had been drafted and sent overseas. She worried about his safety. I went to the cabin to spend a few weeks and keep her company. We played cards, hiked and I read to her *Lovey Mary* and *Mrs. Wiggs of the Cabbage Patch*, two humorous books authored by Alice Hegan Rice, and it was wonderful to see again a smile on her face and a light return to her eyes.

Laura June Kenny

My wonderful Gram Shaffer, whose company I loved.

One day that summer, Gram asked if I was up to hiking down Kagel Canyon to see an old movie star who lived about a mile away. As we approached the small home of the actress, I noticed the windows had very dark blinds, shutting out all daylight. When our hostess answered the door and opened it for us, she held her hand to her eyes to shade them from the light. We entered a room so dark one had to stand for a bit for eyes to adjust to the darkness. In the dimmest of light we found seats and she told us that her years of working under the bright stage lights used for movie-making had ruined her sight and she could not stand anything but the almost total darkness in which she lived. She prepared tea for us, but I will never know how she managed to make and serve it to us before we left that day. Whenever I see present-day star, Jack Nicholson, sporting his usual dark glasses, I wonder if the lighting used for his films brought about a similar, but less severe, condition for him.

At summer's end, when I was driven at night by Lee and Carl to the new home Mother had purchased, I was struck by the fragrance given off by a giant oak tree in the back yard. I could not see the new house nor neighborhood, but oh, the perfume of that oak filled the hot night air. And I was to learn that Woodland Hills is one of the hottest places in the San Fernando Valley. When I awoke next day, I discovered that "Girard," later called Woodland Hills, had been a planned community that never got off the ground floor because of the Depression. Apparently, even though it had been laid out with sidewalks, driveways and street lamps in the late twenties, — in 1943, — it held only two dozen homes scattered here and there. Ours was a fairly new pre-war house with two bedrooms and an attached garage.

Behind our new home, a block away, was stationed a company of soldiers with anti-aircraft equipment aimed at the skies. And behind them was an abandoned golf course, then high with weeds, also part of the ill-fated planning for the Girard development. Living at 21308 Providencia St. meant that Joyce and I would have to take a school bus to the one and only elementary school in the western part of the Valley. It was located in Canoga Park. Woodland Hills sported only a service station and a drug store, which housed the local post office. The pharmacist served as the postmaster.

The nearest grocery store was a **Safeway** in Canoga Park, and the nearest butcher shop was up a hill in a stopping place on Ventura Boulevard, called Calabasas. Without a car and Mother's being able to drive, nothing would do but for me to learn, at age twelve, to ride a bike. Otherwise, we would not eat! Mother found a second-hand Western Flyer boy's bike, which I learned to mount as gracefully as a girl can get into position on one.

Mother also enrolled me in a Saturday Cotillion dancing program. Turning thirteen, I took a liking to one of the two Goodrow brothers, Marvin, with whom I polished up my rendition of the waltz, the fox trot and the rhumba. Sadly, Marvin didn't have eyes for me, but his younger brother Donald did.

When I came to Canoga Park Elementary, one of the last Kindergarten-through-grade-eight schools in the Los Angeles city system, I was supposed to be in the latter half of the seventh grade, due to graduate from eighth grade a year and a half later. But again I was "skipped," and missed the whole bottom half of eighth grade. I was an avid reader, reading more than a book a week and haunting the Canoga Park library. I loved school and my teacher, Elmore K. Miller. Her husband was in the service overseas and she had a son. She told me that, as she drove me on Fridays to the end of the "Red Car" line in Reseda. For when I was to spend a weekend with Mommie Winslow at the Chateau, it was Mrs. Miller who would drive me to the place where I could board the streetcar for Hollywood. Then very early Monday mornings, I would leave the Chateau and go to the Greyhound Station, a few blocks away, there to board a bus that would take me back to Woodland Hills, just in time to get the school bus. What saddened me at the bus station, week after week, was to see a wife or mother tearfully bidding goodbye to a sailor or soldier who had been home "on leave."

But my three brothers didn't come home on leave. Paul was aboard a ship somewhere in the Merchant Marine, and Roger and Chester were stationed in England. My Mother knew exactly where Roger was, for he and she had identical map books, and they had devised a plan whereby she could know his location in spite of wartime censorship. He would write her a V-mail letter on the day of the month that corresponded to the page to which she was to turn. With the v-mail form underneath the map page, and with its being matched corner to corner in the top left-hand corner of the map, he would then stick a pin through the name of the town where he was stationed. When Mother would receive the V-mail, by searching it for the pin prick, and matching it to her map, she could approximate the location where Roger was serving in an intelligence unit. Thus we knew he was safely ensconced at Oxford, England through much of World War II. And after D Day, June 6, 1944, Chet would soon go off to France.

That year in Woodland Hills was one of relative peace between Mother and myself. Only once did she fly into a rage because she thought I had acted inappropriately at a lunch she had given for a retired actor from the Motion Picture Fund Home nearby. He was Lionel Belmore. He enjoyed conversing with me, and later Mother would say I had monopolized the conversation and upstaged her participation. I only thought I was answering his many questions. He was the one and only and the last guest from the Home whom Mother invited for a meal.

When Grandmother Reese suffered a stroke in the spring of that year, after she was hospitalized, Mother brought her to our house until she was able to return to live with Uncle Horace in Hollywood. I loved having her near again, though she had become deaf with the stroke and temporarily could not speak. But she could write, and when I once asked her in writing, if she needed "the vesel," in other words, the bed-pan, she corrected my spelling of the sickroom container in her always beautiful handwriting. Dad was making a good salary with defense work, so Mother hired a housekeeper to lighten her load of caring for Grandmother. Though Honore Burtch was herself elderly, she was a fabulous cook, kept the house spotless and smelling wonderfully of ironed clothes and delicious things in the oven.

Weekends I didn't go to Mommie Winslow's, I spent roaming the vacant Woodland Hills on horseback. There were fire trails I could ride and view the sheep grazing the grassy, vacant hillsides. For two dollars, a gentle horse would be mine for the afternoon that followed a morning of chores done for Mother, — riding to get groceries or meat, picking up the mail, mowing the lawn, or killing one of the chickens she kept and stripping it of feathers. I had read in one of the books that if you put an ice pick into a chicken's brain, it would die immediately, then you could chop off its head. There would be no unnerving "running around" afterwards. I became somewhat adept at this manner of slaughtering, and wonder now I had the will to do it! After Honore came to work for us, she took over the bloody chore, and made the most luscious chicken pot pie and chicken dumplings!

Present-day dwellers of the San Fernando Valley would not recognize the western part of the Valley as it was in those wartime years. Canoga Avenue, now with high-rises on either side, was once a two-lane paved road overhung with pepper trees from Ventura Boulevard north to Sherman Way. Horse ranches lined it also, as I rode this length on my bicycle to get groceries at the Safeway.

I had a special friend that year. Her name was Tenita Mantz, daughter of the famed movie stunt pilot, Paul Mantz. Tenita and her family lived high atop one of the Woodland Hills in a home with a view and a swimming pool. Mr. Mantz fixed hamburgers and hot dogs for us on the barbecue when he would be home from his consulting tasks for the studios, making training films for wartime pilots. He was dashing to look at and charming, as no other friend's father I had ever met, except Roslyn's.

After D-Day in early June, it was graduation time for our small class of eighth graders. Several of our class gave speeches for the occasion and mine was on air transport, expected to mushroom in size when the war would eventually end.

(from l. to r.) Mother, myself and Mama Lee, on graduation day from grade eight.

No sooner had school ended than Mother decided to send us off to live again with Lee and Carl while she would join Dad, who was now working in San Francisco. The house, so newly bought, would be rented out. I was never privy to the farming out arrangements that were made with Mama Lee and Daddy Carl. I just know that there we were in El Monte again, Joyce and I, sharing the bedroom with the twin beds and signing up for school in the fall. While Joyce would begin second grade, I would take the college preparatory course at El Monte Union High School, now burgeoning with three thousand students, going to school in staggered shifts, early morning or late morning. The late jockey, Willie Shoemaker, was in my huge freshman class, though I did not know him then.

Lee saw to it that I had nice clothes besides those given me by Aunt Grace Kahn and Mommie Winslow. She or Daddy Carl drove me to the dances held summer evenings in the huge gymnasium. Though I was new, and a wallflower, — no one asking me to dance, — I loved every moment when the Big Band sound was in the air.

El Monte High was special. The original school had all but one building destroyed by the 1933 Long Beach earthquake. The W.P.A. had rebuilt the school on more spacious grounds with superb architecture and planning just prior to the war. The school boasted one of the finest stages and auditoriums in the San Gabriel Valley, and enlisted first class music teachers among its staff. Hal Brown was in charge of instrumental music and Lois Wells headed the vocal music department. Outstanding even that early in her career, Miss Wells would go on to become "the grandmother" of all vocal music teachers throughout California. Twenty-five years later, my older daughter would have a vocal music teacher in high school, one trained extensively in music education by Lois Wells. I treasure the latter having taught us the score for *Showboat*, as well as so many other standards such as Gershwin's music from *Porgy and Bess*.

The real highlight of my two years at El Monte High School was being in the English class, both years, of Vivian Williams. Though Lee and Carl provided a warm and comfortable home in which to live, their household was not one where intellect was honored or encouraged. There were few, if any books, and reading consisted of scanning the daily paper. Previous summers, when staying with the Ingrams, I had obtained a local library card and read the best sellers, *The Egg and I* and *A Tree Grows in Brooklyn*. As well, I had read every Kathleen Norris novel on which I could lay hands, and some of L. M. Montgomery's *Anne of Green Gables* series.

Vivian and I made an instant connection, starting with our sharing the same last name. And she had a son, Richard, who looked like a young Tyrone Power. He helped me with a science project that first year, but we never went on any dates, just on day fishing trips with his mom and dad. It was the quality and depth of Vivian's teaching that so inspired the thirteen-year-old mind I brought to class each day. We read all the classics featured in college preparatory English classes: *Silas Marner*, Shakespeare's *Julius Ceasar*, and Dickens' *Tale of Two Cities*. Beyond that, Vivian introduced me to anthologies of writers, and in our private student-teacher conferences, she encouraged my launching out to write creatively. Our whole class was grounded in the fundamentals of diagramming language, or what others called "parsing."

I am forever grateful that Vivian Williams entered me in speech contests, some of which I won, even competing with a future Congressman and judge, Chuck Wiggins. When I had won one Lion's Club speech contest, I was asked to deliver my speech at two assemblies of the whole El Monte High student body. This meant I had to stand before two groups of fifteen hundred students and speak from memory for several minutes. I remember thinking, as I stood there in my corduroy jumper and white blouse, "If I get through this, I will never be afraid to speak in public again." And I never have been since that day!

Through the two years, Vivian and I formed a deep bond that went well beyond student and teacher. "You are so like Emily in *Our Town*," she would say.

"What do you mean?" I would ask.

Then my teacher would quote the words that the character Emily speaks to the Stage Manager character in that classic play by Thornton Wilder: "Oh, earth, you're too wonderful for anyone to realize you.....Do any human beings realize life while they live it—every, every minute?" It took many years, and many life experiences before I would understand the profundity of Emily's question, and the simplicity and reality of the Stage Manager's response: "No—Saints and poets maybe—they do some."

Vivian bought tickets to Saturday matinees at the Biltmore Theater in downtown Los Angeles, and she would drive the two of us from El Monte to one of the parking lots near Pershing Square. Before the theater performance, we had lunch at the downtown Bullock's Tea Room, where she had served as a waitress, putting herself through U.C.L.A. twenty years before. We saw several plays during those two years, and once I took her backstage to meet an actress I knew who lived at the Chateau.

The most memorable theater occasion was when the wide-smiling actor, Joe E. Brown, starred in the play *Harvey* and following his performance, I wrote a note of thanks to him. He was gracious enough to answer in his own hand: "Thanks for your note, and the very nice thoughts of me that you expressed. To know that I have been an influence for good on youngsters like you makes me very happy. I hope your life will be filled with happiness. Sincerely, Joe E. Brown." I liked the way he penned his letter e, much like that letter when written in Greek, and I adopted that style immediately after.

Mommie Winslow's admonition to always write a note of thanks, when something thrills or even just pleases you, bore such fruit, as I was to learn time and again.

Soon after I started high school, I read in the daily paper that Chico Marx had a band and was performing on the Orpheum circuit as a stage act to compliment the movie theater's feature film. Mama Lee and I took the "Red Car" from El Monte to the downtown Los Angeles Orpheum Theater. When his part of the stage performance was over, I sent a note backstage, reminding him who I was, and how much I wanted to see him again. The usher returned to where we were seated and said, "Follow me." We were taken to Chico's tiny dressing room where he had removed his wig and was resting.

As we entered his small space, I spoke first. "I still have that camera you gave me," I told Daddy Max's favorite poker player. For his part, Chico spoke endearingly about what a wonderful man Max Winslow had been, and what a faithful friend Max had proved to be, over so many years.

"I miss him, too, Laura June. What a guy!" Chico looked wistful, shook my hand and bade us goodbye. Whereas the other Marx Brothers, Groucho and Harpo, had stashed away and wisely invested the money they had earned making movies, their piano-playing brother would have to find entertainment work for almost all of the rest of his life because of his compulsion to gamble.

The spring of 1945 began with the death of a former *Little Rascal*, Bobby "Wheezer" Hutchins, killed in a World War II military plane crash around the time of his twentieth birthday. "Wheezer" had appeared in fifty-eight *Our Gang* shorts from the time he was two until he was eight years old. He was a youngster who spanned the transition from silent movies to those with sound. But his death made little news in a world that was seeing an end to the war, as the Allied Forces, from both directions, bore down upon Nazi Germany. Then President Roosevelt died at Warm Springs, Georgia, in mid-April, the only President I could remember, and one I revered like a national father-figure. As Germany moved closer to unconditional surrender in early May, world leaders had gathered in San Francisco to form the United Nations. Our social studies class followed closely all these events, and I made a scrapbook about the emergent U.N.

Then it was summer, and I would go to Gram's for the first part of the summer, which would be my last summer in Kagel Canyon. Bill Jones had married and his wife had come to stay with Gram until he was discharged from the service. Gram and I could not enjoy the level of closeness we had known in previous summers with a third party, and a vegetarian, occupying the household. I concentrated on "getting a tan," drenching myself with peanut oil, and lying out on Gram's secluded patio.

In August, Mother and Dad sent train tickets for Joyce and me, so that we might come spend a few weeks with them in San Francisco. It was our first trip by train, and a porter was tipped at Los Angeles Union Station to see to it we arrived safely. Housing was scarce in 1945, but Mother and Dad had moved from a hotel room to a basement apartment, high atop one of San Francisco's many hills. Part of that vacation was spent out at the Russian River, north of San Francisco, where redwoods were plentiful and the river warm. But the most memorable day was V-J Day, when the Japanese war forces unconditionally surrendered to the United States, out in the Pacific, on a battleship named the *USS Missouri*.

We had planned to meet my Dad, after his day of work, downtown on Market Street. When Mother, Joyce and I arrived at the appointed meeting-place we were joined by thousands of people celebrating the victory announcement. Servicemen, especially sailors who were docked at

San Francisco, filled the streets, as did civilians, glad the war had ceased. It was truly a crushing bit of humanity, and we could hardly stay with our Mother or at her side. I was grabbed by several young men, wanting to celebrate with a kiss, but my Mother said sternly, "No, you don't. She's only fourteen!" We never found my Dad but since no streetcars were running, we hiked up Market Street, past the U. S. Mint Building, where inside they continued to punch out pennies.

When Joyce and I returned to El Monte for the start of school in September, we were unprepared for the turmoil that had transpired in Lee's and Carl's life during our absence. We were, as only a fourteen and eight-year-old could be, unaware that the Ingrams marriage was "on the rocks." Lee had taken to drinking heavily, and Carl was sick of it. She picked me up at school one day and took me off in her little coupe to a side-street to tell me Carl had packed a bag and left the house, "moved out," she said. She was heart-broken and devastated. With the naiveté of a teenager, I suggested she take up Christian Science, the religion whose local Sunday School I had attended since she had first enrolled me many years before.

Desperate as she was, Lee took my advice, gave up smoking and drinking, abandoned drinking coffee, (her mainstay), bought a Bible and Christian Science books, read and studied them day and night, and later would say, "And a little child shall lead them." Lee had unflagging faith that Carl would return to her, even though he had filed for the first stage of the divorce process, the interlocutory decree, then prevailing in California courts.

It would be many months before Carl came back to a forgiving Lee, who had watched him spend nights at a woman neighbor's house, just down the street. In the meantime, my two brothers, Roger and Chester, returned from Europe and were discharged from the armed services. While becoming reestablished as civilians, and with no Los Angeles home to which to return, they asked if they might stay at Lee's. She was glad to accommodate them, and gave them the use of the two twin Murphy beds in her den. I loved having my brothers back home, Roger helping me in my struggle with algebra homework, and Chester taking me to see my first opera, a production of *Aida*.

During his brief stay at Lee's, Chester also took me to see an elderly lady in Hollywood, whose lawns he had once mowed. The night we visited, we also met her niece, Agnes Newton Keith, author of *Land Below the Wind*. Ms. Keith had only recently returned to California with her husband and son, after the three were liberated from a Japanese concentration camp. My brother and I were shocked by her gaunt, frail appearance, and she smoked incessantly. Later that year, I heard that she was writing a book about her internment experience, *Three Came Home*. In 1950, Claudette Colbert would star in the movie with the same name as the book.

On the first night Roger came to El Monte, he was still in uniform, looking a handsome age twenty-one. I was scheduled to attend a nighttime high school football game with my assistant Girl Scout leader and her sister. I asked if Roger could accompany us, and off we went. How proud I was, at the singing of the national anthem, when Roger stood tall, and soberly sang with his beautiful voice. Little did I know that night that I had facilitated a meeting that would later produce an almost sixty-year marriage.

When Chester found work quickly and bought a car, he moved out of the El Monte home. He wanted to return to his art studies, and his former teacher, Mr. Lukits, lived in Los Angeles. But Roger stayed on, beginning to date the assistant Girl Scout leader, and finding work in her father's nearby lumberyard. Then late one night, he came into my room and awakened me to tell me he had asked this beautiful young woman of twenty to marry him. "What did she say?" I asked. His beaming smile wordlessly told me her answer had been a resounding "Yes." Wedding plans were being made, and his future mother-in-law found a spare room for him to occupy in the meantime. He moved out, and left Joyce and me with a newly restored marriage, for Carl dropped his divorce proceedings and returned to live with Lee. Carl now joined Lee in her faithful study of Christian Science and both joined the local Christian Science church. All was harmony and peace, but not for long!

When my Mother, in San Francisco, learned of the wedding planned for the summer of 1946, she descended upon the Ingrams' household like a black torrent of rage and fury. She barely greeted my sister and me that April evening, then sent us off to our bedroom, for she said she had something to discuss with Lee and Carl. The "discussion" went on for many hours, until early morning, and from my bed, in terror and sadness, I listened to her berating Lee and Carl, blaming them for tearing her family apart.

It seems Mother had wanted to move back to the house in Woodland Hills. My Dad, she said, would return to Southern California, and we would all be "one happy family" together again! Mother told the Ingrams that she would have us pack up our belongings in the morning and accompany her back to San Francisco. Then I heard Lee and Carl plead with her that I be allowed to stay on until the close of school, for I had scheduled speech contests and I was nearly a straight A student. The move, in mid-semester, would be too disruptive, especially since I was taking the college preparatory course. Mother finally capitulated on my leaving just then, but packed up Joyce's things in the morning and took her to San Francisco.

I remember little of that spring except that I would be fitted for a bridesmaid's dress for Roger's wedding, and that I once, on a happy day, accompanied his bride-to-be as she selected her trousseau in downtown Los Angeles stores. It was a spring of sadness as I said goodbye to friends I knew I might never see again. And there were the almost weekly letters from Mother that sent shivers up my spine when I saw her handwriting on the outside envelope, before I even read the letters' contents. They were a series of written tirades against Lee and Carl, against me, against my brother Roger and his future wife. "At least, when I have to go to live with her, I won't have to receive these letters," I consoled myself.

When school ended, I was whisked to the house in Woodland Hills, where the renters had left for the summer. I would not see Lee and Carl again until the day of the wedding, for in spite of Mother, they were on the guest list. I could, of course, not see Gram again, and I missed being with her at the cabin in Kagel Canyon. I was allowed to see my cousin Shirley Kibbee for the last time, and I often went in to Hollywood to spend time with Mommie Winslow. The previous summer she had introduced me to the blonde athletic son of a Christian Science practitioner. He was Carroll Sax, and his father was a producer at Warner Brothers studio.

It was a long bus ride in from Woodland Hills to Carroll's home, a shorter ride if I was coming from Mommie Winslow's. Leaving transportation at the corner of Hollywood and Highland, I would enter the old Hollywood Hotel, a landmark at the northwest corner of that intersection, and powder my nose, comb my hair and put on lipstick in one of the hotel's restrooms, then I would be off to spend the day with Carroll. There was a pool at his Hollywood Boulevard apartment complex and I loved to swim and dive with him. After a day at the pool, his parents would take us for dinner at the Hollywood Roosevelt Hotel, and maybe on to the Hollywood Bowl.

On one of that summer's visits, I asked Carroll who was in his classes at Hollywood High. I learned that he knew many of my old friends from Gardner Street School days, especially Deborah Marshall, whose home I had loved to visit. Then he asked me if I knew another girl who had attended Gardner Street with me. Not only did I know her, but she had been in one episode of the *Little Rascals* with me. "I am sorry to tell you this," Carroll said, "but she is now a prostitute on Hollywood Boulevard." We were all, — Carroll, that girl and myself, —only fifteen years old at the time he relayed that sad bit of news. That benighted little blonde was already living out an aspect of what later would be called, "The Curse of the Little Rascals."

I tried to spend as much time with Mommie Winslow as I could, as the summer progressed, for I knew it would be a long time before we could be together again. One night we went to a little dinner party at the Reingold's out in Beverly Hills. Mommie Winslow said, "Laura June, I want you to meet one of Daddy Max's dearest friends from our days in New York." She took me over to a balding man whose back was turned toward us, and she called to him, "Jolie." He turned to face us. "Honey, this is Mr. Jolson," Mommie Winslow said, smiling broadly. "Al, this our girl, Laura June." Little did I realize that the next spring I would see his life story , in living color, in a movie. He was in town to sing the lyrics for *The Jolson Story*. We made "small talk" and Al Jolson introduced us to his new and very young wife.

A few days before Roger's wedding, Mommie Winslow asked me to go and spend the night with her ailing cousin, the lady I called Aunt Lena. Her apartment was very close to the little cottage on Camerford Street where my Grandmother Reese lived with her brother, "Unkie" Horace. Although Grandmother could not hear a word I said to her, she had, from her experience as an elocution teacher, become adept at reading lips and so we conversed for an hour or two on that sunny August morning. When I was ready to head back to Woodland Hills, my eighty-two-year-old Grandmother walked me out to the sidewalk and stood there waving to me until I turned the corner. She knew, and I did, too, that it would be the last time we laid eyes on each other!

While my bridesmaid's dress was a floor-length light blue, and I had a picture voile hat to match, my Mother chose to wear black for her middle son's wedding. She bought a simple black crepe dress of street length, and focused all her attention on a hat for the occasion. Her friend, Mrs. Lady, made a black velvet hat with white lace trim. "Black for a wedding?" Mommie Winslow said, and shook her head in dismay when I told her of the dress, and hat-making preparations.

Then came the wedding rehearsal night in El Monte. The rehearsal went off beautifully, but the ride back to Woodland Hills was a disaster. Chester, or Paul, who by now had returned from service in the Merchant Marine, was driving. I pretended to fall asleep in the back seat, but I could not but overhear my Mother do a repeat performance of the April night at Lee and Carl's: "Lee and Carl are to blame for Roger meeting this girl and wanting to marry her so soon after being discharged." If only Roger had never been taken in as a roomer by Lee, then the wedding of the next day would not be taking place. Mother had made plans to bring us all together, to live under one roof out in Woodland Hills, just as we had briefly, for the last time at 6161 Whitsett Street in North Hollywood, the summer of 1942. And on and on she went, the forty-five miles from El Monte to the west Valley.

The wedding took place the next day without a hitch, even if my Mother grimly shook hands with people in the reception line, and even if I felt sick at my stomach and faint, as I marched down the aisle ahead of my soon-to-be sister-in-law. The reality of leaving the loving and the familiar, and of having to live again under my Mother's roof, was settling in my bones. But youth has the capacity to hope, and I hoped that there would

117

Laura June Kenny

be something good for me in that City by the Bay to which I was soon to depart.

CHAPTER 4

"THE CITY" AND THE UNIVERSITY
1946-51

I looked at the morning-after newspaper pictures of the posh opening of the 1946 gala San Francisco Opera season, with women in ball gowns and men in tuxedos. Then I looked around at the house to which Mother had brought Joyce and me. The contrast was dramatic! Postwar housing in the Bay Area was still scarce. The small frame house at 76 Vernon Street was painted battleship gray. It had been built as "temporary housing" after the San Francisco Earthquake of 1906, probably for a family, as it had three small bedrooms. If you had put a golf ball in the middle of the kitchen, the biggest room in the house, the ball might have rolled to any one of the four corners of that room. I had never lived in such an unevenly floored and decrepit house before. Even Gram's "cabin" was elegant in comparison!

With Mother now working as a teacher of court reporting, and with Dad, at age fifty-four, involved in post-war construction, my parents could afford to send for some of their furniture that had been stored in the Northwest since they left Washington state fourteen years previously. I had my bedroom set that Mommie Winslow had bought for me ten years before, and Mother had the newer dining room suite she had bought for the

Woodland hills house. And the 1928 Maytag ringer washing machine with its square tub found its place on the back porch along with an old-fashioned wooden icebox. That washer and I would become very well acquainted in the next few years!

The first persons I met, on my first day at the new high school, were Avonne Akey and her mother. The three of us were on the 'L' streetcar heading to the street, out in "the Avenues," where the City's newest high school was located. "Bonnie" was new to the area too, having just moved to the West Portal district from New Jersey. We alighted from the streetcar and trudged to the top of the hill where the four-story lone classroom building stood. Abraham Lincoln High had been built at the beginning of World War II, and its auditorium and gymnasium had not yet come into being. For the two years I would attend, our student body would never experience those amenities.

Though the newer high school lacked the spacious grounds and edifices of El Monte Union High School, its student body and teaching staff were much more sophisticated. Fellow classmates were friendly and welcoming, especially Barbara Flaherty, Betty Quent and Kathie Harriman.

I also met another newcomer from Southern California, a girl named Lynn. She and I commiserated about how we missed the Los Angeles area. For four months, together we rode the 19th Avenue bus to school each day. Since Mother allowed no contact whatsoever with Lee and Carl, no letters or phone calls, I felt cut off even more from a physical area that had been my "stomping grounds" for the prior fourteen years.

Radio and routine helped. Since most radio programs at that time originated in Hollywood, I listened to them as I lived out the daily routine. After school, I would come home, wash the breakfast dishes, set the table and begin the dinner preparations. Before it got dark, I walked a few blocks to my sister's school and called for her when her after-school programs ended. Mother and Dad would not return from their jobs until after dark. While Mother worked downtown, on Market Street, Dad's construction projects were in South San Francisco. Both used crowded rush-hour public transportation.

A bright spot in those first few months was meeting Sylvia and Steve Newman at the West Portal Public Library. Like us, they had no car at the time, so we became acquainted riding home on the 'M' car line. The Newmans lived at the other end of the next block, Arch Street. Over the next five years, they were my emotional anchors in the stormy sea of my adolescence and my having to cope with Mother's many unpredictable moods.

Weekends had their routines too. On Saturdays I accompanied Joyce to her three dancing lessons on Market Street: ballet, tap dancing and adagio, (what today is called gymnastics). Her teachers, Stanley Kahn and Pat Mason, were the summertime choreographers for the Ice Follies, for the show's founders, Shipstads and Johnson, brought their troupe to San Francisco each summer to prepare for the new show year that would begin in September.

Sundays we attended the Christian Science Sunday School, returning home afterwards to do chores like getting our clothes ready for the week to come. Mother had washed clothes while we were away in the morning, so they were ironed Sunday afternoons as we listened to radio programs: *One Man's Family*, *The Jack Benny Show*, *Fred Allen*, *The Theater Guild of the Air*, and always, Walter Winchell's staccato newscast.

If the weather were nice, Sylvia and Steve took Joyce and me sightseeing on the bus to get us acquainted with San Francisco. Our destinations might be Fisherman's Wharf, Coit Tower, the zoo, Seal Rocks, the de Young Museum or the aquarium. We usually ended our touring afternoon at the massive Golden Gate Park

San Francisco is an air-conditioned city with a mean temperature of about 58 degrees F. Having come from Southern California's warmth, I was cold all that first year, my "blood adjusting to the cooler weather," I was told.

My three brothers and sister-in-law came up for Thanksgiving, a little break of "family togetherness." Then came Christmas vacation when Roger and his wife returned and took me down the Peninsula to spend a few days with the Forrest Barnes family, including my former playmate from Laurel Avenue days, fourteen-year-old Christopher. The Barnes family had moved north from Hollywood to a "Sky Ranch" high atop the hills of the San Francisco peninsula, a quieter venue for their writing. That ranch had been the prototype of the ranch which radio-writer Carleton E. Morris used as a rural backdrop for his *One Man's Family* broadcasts. Christopher took me horseback riding, and I was not the rider I had been only three years before. The horse ran away with me, and stopped just short of a gate, almost pitching me out of the saddle and into the air!

Of course, Mother was stressed out, working long hours and commuting from the outskirts of the city to downtown employment and back again at day's end. Dictating to budding court reporters all day, — five days a week, eight hours a day, — wore out her eyesight, her voice and her emotional reserves. Besides, she was going through "The Change of Life." She had no patience for how I cooked, washed dishes, scrubbed the bathtub, shopped, ironed clothes or did errands for her. Whatever I did was never good enough to satisfy her! Always I should have known better than to do what I did!

But I was not the only object of Mother's ire. Never before had my bedroom been adjacent to my parents' room. Now, night after night, I fell asleep hearing Mother berate my Dad. Sometimes I would awaken from sleep to the sounds of her anger still being vented toward him. She would recall, in vivid detail, events and instances that had happened ten or twenty years before. Dad never responded to a single charge she made. How he could get up the next morning and go to work I never could understand!

Sad to say, Mother forced me to write an unkind letter to Roger, saying things I didn't want to say to him, words she dictated. Roger's wife wrote back to me, telling me how deeply I had hurt him. About that time I wrote to my eldest brother Chester about Mother's demands and her harangues. His reply to me, in a letter, which I opened before Mother came home from work, was terse: "I am sorry for your situation, but our mother has 'cancer of the soul!'" At least one person verbalized for me what I was enduring and witnessing on a daily basis.

Lynn, my girl friend and former Los Angeles resident, returned to the Southland suddenly in January. I felt bereft, and now became very depressed. I wore no make-up at school and dressed my hair in one long braid formed at the back of my head. Walking the steep hills of San Francisco was sometimes the only relief I could find for the gloom all about me. But breathing deeply those breezes from the ocean, I ended up strengthening my legs. As always, for me, Emerson's edict would ring true: "A certain *compensation* balances every gift and every defect."

My precious Grandmother Reese, whom I had seen for the last time the summer before, died in January in her eighty-fourth year, in Los Angeles. Mother left for a few days to tend to her burial. I was so grateful that Grandmother and I had spent a few hours together that warm August morning. That gratitude brought comfort and closure. Nothing had ever passed between Grandmother and myself but pure love and delight!

One day that winter of 1947, my sister Joyce and I were practicing her dance steps in the big kitchen, and I felt dreadfully ill. We both broke out with the chicken pox. While her lesions lasted only a few days, I was very sick for three weeks, and missed school. The truant officer came to the front door, and did not believe how ill I had been. So I lifted my shirt to show him the still oozing lesions on my abdomen. By phone, my girl friends at Lincoln High had kept me up-to-date with homework assignments.

I was no sooner enrolled in the second semester of my junior year, when Dad had an industrial accident lifting a heavy metal beam. He ruptured a disc in his lower back. Later he would have surgery for the condition, one of the first of the ruptured disc back operations of the post-war era.

For a short while after the surgery, he was in a ward of Franklin Hospital, where I went after school each day to help feed him his supper. Sometimes I finished off his tray of food, for what he was served was better than what supper would be that night when I would finally arrive home.

Seeing him late each day was a high spot that better prepared me to face Mother later on.

Several weeks into his recovery, his ward-mates taught him the fundamentals of baseball, for the whole ward listened to the games on the radio. Dad thus developed a late but lifelong love of baseball! He who was born in October of 1892 would come to revere his natal month because, each successive year, it meant the coming of the World Series!

Then it was time for Dad to return home, but he was in a body-cast and had to remain in bed. He needed daily care. I dropped out of chemistry, physical education and chorus, attending Lincoln High only in the afternoons, where I studied Geometry, Spanish, English and American History. Mornings I did the washing and hung it out to dry, then fed and bathed and bed-panned my bedfast Dad. I left for school each day at noon, making sure the radio was nearby so he could reach it. That enabled him to listen to all the news and sportscasts he could dial to. He was "a political junkie," a trait I inherited from him, along the way!

A boy in my geometry class always asked me to show him my homework, saying he was too busy to complete his assignment every afternoon, playing golf with his dad, a "pro" at a San Francisco course. My classmate was named Kenny Venturi, who later became a CBS sportscaster and earlier, a winner of many golf tournaments.

However Mother behaved at home, outside, —especially at her workplace, the court-reporting school, —she was the paragon of patience and concern for her pupils. She used her lunch-hours and after-school hours to give extra dictation to students who were falling behind. As expressions of thanks from her pupils, Mother would receive tickets to plays and other events, so Mother took me to see *Pygmalion*, with Gertrude Lawrence, and the *Song of Norway*. True, I was out of Hollywood, and was never going to be in the movies, but oh, how I loved legitimate theater! That year I devoured the biographies of actresses like Katherine Cornell and Helen Hayes.

One day, sometime that first year of living at home with my parents, Mother and I were scrubbing the walls of the kitchen prior to its being re-painted and spruced up. We were working side-by-side and easy conversation flowed between us. She began to share something of her own history and her own feelings, but none of her dialogue was tinged with the usual bitterness and animosity. Her observations had the ring of peaceful objectivity. There was genuine rapport between us. It was as if an immense veil had been lifted and I was being privileged to see who she really was. I thought to myself, "This is what it is like when I talk with Mama Lee or Mommie Winslow. Isn't this wonderful? I wish we could talk like this some more." But no sooner had those thoughts crossed my mind, than the veil suddenly descended once more, and she took up a different train of conversation, filled with vitriol and criticism.

Though Mama Lee abided by Mother's edict that she was not to write to me, that didn't deter her from airmailing me, from time to time, boxes of the camellias that grew all around the El Monte home where once I had lived, and was so loved. Those beautiful blossoms of white and pink and red helped to get me through that hectic spring.

Then I turned sixteen in June. At some level I decided it would be a year to be "sweet sixteen." I read as many of Shakespeare's plays as I could get my hands on. Also I took swimming lessons at the Fleishhacker salt-water pool, adjacent to the San Francisco Zoo. My sister was in a weekly summer program run by the Camp Fire Girls, so I accompanied her and assisted the leader in the various activities.

A highlight of the late summer was a visit from Los Angeles of my friend Phyllis Lundine. She spent a whole week at our home, and I showed her all around San Francisco. Sylvia and Steve had schooled me well in the beauties San Francisco had to offer residents and visitors alike!

Through connections at Sunday School, I obtained baby-sitting jobs, earning enough money to shop for school clothes in late August. I would need to appear and dress better, for during the summer I snagged my first real boy-friend, Bliss Stanley, a Sunday School acquaintance and classmate at Lincoln. Bliss worked in an ice-cream store after school, drove his family's old car, and took me boating on Lake Merced and to concerts at

125

Stern Grove. We attended little theater productions and baseball games of the San Francisco Seals. (The Giants were not to arrive for another decade!)

Bliss was a "big man on campus," serving in student government, so I drew near to the fringes of the "in" crowd at high school, though I was never really a part of it. With just babysitting money, and with Dad disabled and not working, I could never afford the "white buck" oxfords and sets of cashmere sweaters my classmates sported. But I had a "secret weapon" where formal dances and proms were concerned!

The Christmas of 1947, Mother allowed me to return to Southern California for a week. I spent several days with Mommie Winslow in Hollywood as well as a few days with my brother Roger and his wife in El Monte. While at Roger's, I longed to see Lee and Carl Ingram, so close at hand. It had been a year and a half since Mother had issued the order that I could not go to the Ingrams' home. But I had a plan. I asked Roger to take me to the home of my former English teacher, Vivian Williams, who also lived in El Monte. From there I called Mama Lee and Daddy Carl, and they rushed right over to see me. We had about an hour's visit face-to-face. I had seen them, yes, but I could say I did not visit their home!

While I stayed at Mommie Winslow's, the two of us visited Aunt Rose Cohn for an afternoon, at her Chateau Marmont apartment. Aunt Rose had formal attire to give me, gowns she had worn but once or twice. I had an interesting encounter with one of Aunt Rose's pals during that visit. Her friend was Lillian Paley, a wealthy matron, and in-law of CBS head, William Paley. As I talked of how the new formals would enhance my social life, Mrs. Paley asked me very seriously, "Do you have a boy-friend, Laura June?"

"Yes," I answered shyly.

"Is he nice to you, I mean kind to you, Laura June?"

"Oh, yes, he's very good to me, Mrs. Paley!" I assured her.

"That's the most important thing, —kindness," she said, and there came over her face such a look of longing and sadness, that I remember it well to this day! Instantly, even my sixteen-year-old awareness made note that "money isn't everything," and that happiness is not always found with a famous name and great riches to fall back upon.

Aunt Rose had given me a white chiffon ball gown and an iridescent taffeta gown. But I also took back to San Francisco two other formals, one of blue net, and an Empire-style gown of gold damask, the gifts of Aunt Grace Kahn and her daughter Irene, then married to Groucho Marx's son Arthur. Until these gowns had come my way, all I could wear to formal affairs was my bridesmaid's gown left over from Roger's wedding two summers before. The sophistication of San Francisco spilled over into the dances of the City's high schools. The Sir Francis Drake Hotel, the Palace Hotel, the Yacht Club in the Marina, — all these were venues for school formal dances.

By the fall of 1947 and winter of 1948, Dad was somewhat improved, and because he stayed home while Mother worked, he now did the housework, the washing and much of the cooking. I had less to do around the house and thus could enjoy something of a school social life in my senior year. I joined Tri-Y, an after-school girls' club, and the Debate Club, and I took part in many speech contests, as I had done in El Monte. On Saturdays, if I were not attending a debate tournament somewhere, I frequently ushered at the magnificent San Francisco Opera House matinees, taking in both operas and musical comedies. When I assisted in the Library at school, the school Librarian insisted that I make application to attend the University of California at Berkeley the following fall. With family financial resources almost nil, I had been planning to attend San Francisco City College after graduation.

Then, around Christmastime, Mother developed a massive fibroid tumor and quit her work. She had surgery and was off work for some time. Now we had only $30.00 a week to live on, a kind of Workmen's Compensation Dad received. Our usual dinner fare consisted of beans and carrots, and occasionally fish. I put on twelve pounds.

My brother Roger was studying court-reporting in Los Angeles, and thus my Mother learned of an opening for a teacher of court-reporting there. She left to make her housing headquarters at our former Woodland Hills home, renting a room there from the tenants who had occupied the home since 1946. But the distance between downtown Los Angeles and Woodland Hills was so far, transportation so expensive and so infrequent, that she ended up spending a lot of nights at downtrodden downtown hotels or alternatively sleeping in the open-all-night Hollywood Theater on Hollywood Boulevard.

That spring, I was heavily into speechmaking and debates, as well as dates and pre-graduation festivities with Bliss. I wanted to be slender for graduation, so I ate with the family only sparingly and at suppertime. My other two meals consisted of Ry-Krisp and applesauce and non-fat milk. I slimmed down to 112 pounds.

Three events capped high school graduation for me. I heard in April that I had been accepted as a freshman undergraduate at the University of California at Berkeley. (I can't remember her name, but I will be forever grateful to the Librarian, who, the previous fall, urged me to apply for admission to U.C., Berkeley.) Then in May, I received a notice that I would receive a State of California Scholarship that would take care of the first year's tuition and the cost of some books. Tuition for "Cal" in 1948 was $35.00 per semester. The scholarship was for $150.00. Finally, late in May, I was selected to be one of the three valedictorians for my graduating class of just over 300 students.

The big night came on June 16, and our family, — my parents and my two brothers, Paul and Chet, —attended the graduation exercises at George Washington High School Auditorium. I felt six feet tall as I marched into the auditorium to the strains of "Pomp and Circumstance." After the ceremonies, twin brothers in our class hosted an all-night party. There was dancing, but no drinking, however, neither Bliss nor I could stay awake after three a.m., so Bliss drove me home. The beautiful chapter of my life called high school was over. I would turn the page to a new kind of learning, come September!

Myself, in high school, wearing the blue net gown.

It saddened me that Mommie Winslow could not come north to attend my graduation, but I understood. As always, she had her cousin Lena to look after, with daily visits to her cousin's nursing home a priority in her life. She wrote me a letter, which said in part, "I am sorry, darling, that I am unable to come up for the graduation, to see my little girl that we are all so proud of…..I regret so much that I won't hear your speech. Be sure to keep a copy for me, as you know that will grace my treasure book.....All your Aunts, — Jane, Lena, Rose, Alice, Grace and countless others, — join in heartiest congratulations and send much love.....All my love, Devotedly, Mommie Winslow."

The summer of 1948 was a time of celebration. Mother and Dad bought me my first wristwatch, — a Wittnauer, —for graduation. Uncle Moe Reingold, helped to select it for them, back in his Beverly Hills jewelry store. But Mother's biggest present was relenting about my not being allowed to see Lee and Carl. I took all the gifts of money I had received from Mommie Winslow and my "Aunts" in Hollywood, and went to Southern California for the summer.

How wonderful it was to go back to the El Monte house and be immersed in the love of the Ingrams again. For my graduation, they had bought me Samsonite luggage, and we three spent some happy hours at Catalina Island where they had honeymooned nineteen years before.

Daddy Carl and me, on Catalina Island, summer 1948.

I spent considerable time also with Mommie Winslow, the first such long visit in two years. She, who had never attended college, but educated herself by having read the whole series of *The Pocket University*, now shared with me her love of higher learning. Late at night, with me seated at her bedside, the two of us discussed books and authors that had made a difference in her life. There was Oscar Wilde, George Eliot, Goethe and the Romain Rolland trilogy on *Jean-Christophe*. Ellin Berlin's second novel, *Lace Curtain*, had just been published that year and Mommie Winslow put it into my hands to read on that visit. "Laura June, I want you to read what it is like with mixed marriages. Mine has worked out well, and so has Ellin's to Irving, but most have the problems Ellin points to."

I went with Tillie each day, on the bus, to visit with her cousin Lena, who was in a nursing home near Vermont Avenue. Mommie Winslow told me often that her dream for my college years, those college years that she and Daddy Max had so wanted to make possible, could not be fulfilled. In those post-war years of the 1940s, when there was no Medicare, Mommie Winslow assumed for seven years the full financial responsibility for her cousin's nursing home care, after Aunt Lena had suffered several strokes.

Many evenings I went with Aunt Rose to the Hollywood Bowl. She had season tickets and we sat in her box for those wonderful "concerts under the stars." During one of these concerts, at intermission, Aunt Rose and I approached a tall, ruggedly handsome man in a camel's hair coat. Aunt Rose called to him, "Ezio, I want you to meet my niece, Laura June! Laura June, this is Ezio Pinza!" My heart fluttered as we made conversation, for when I had ushered at the San Francisco Opera House, I had heard him sing the lead in *Faust*. And his real-life daughter had appeared with him. Little did I know then that this great singer would, that coming fall, star on Broadway, cast opposite Mary Martin in the smash hit, Rodgers and Hammerstein's *South Pacific*. One of the first long-play 33rpm records I ever bought was the exciting score of that great stage production.

Before graduation, earlier in the spring, when preparing supper and listening to the news, I used to hear insightful news analyses by CBS's Charles Collingwood. He was broadcasting out of Hollywood at radio station KNX for fifteen minutes every weekday. One day, he talked at length about "the marketplace of ideas," and quoted Oliver Wendell Holmes. I was so inspired by the concepts he was putting forward, that I wrote to the broadcaster, asking for a copy of that particular day's broadcast script. I told him I wanted to take ideas from the script and weave them into my graduation valedictory speech. Collingwood promptly sent along the script, asked for a copy of my speech when completed, and invited me to visit him at the Hollywood studio the next time I was in Southern California. "Call my secretary to arrange to see my broadcast," he had written.

The Chateau Elysee was only a ten minute walk from the CBS radio studio at Gower and Sunset, so twice I visited with Charles Collingwood, and after viewing his broadcast, sitting in the booth with the engineer, we went outside to the courtyard and talked at length. He told me he had been a "scholarship bum," attending several colleges. We talked politics because it was the turbulent 1948 summer of several political parties, not only the Democrats and Republicans, but also the Dixiecrats and the Wallace Progressive Party. I asked Charlie how he remained objective and did not insert his own political views into his analyses or commentaries. His reply I'll never forget: "But June, I'm not trying to sell anything!" Today we might term such a Collingwood-rejected sales job as a "spin."

Mother was selling the Woodland Hills home for three times the $3500.00 purchase price she had paid in 1943. Many of the servicemen who had visited or been stationed in Southern California during World War II were now returning as civilians and bringing their families to settle in the San Fernando Valley. I helped Mother pack for shipping some of our belongings, which had been stored for the past four years in the garage. Mommie Winslow had sold the cottage at Alexandria Bay in the Thousand Islands the summer before, gifting me with books and mementoes of her twenty-eight year ownership, the only home she and Daddy Max had ever owned. I listened on the radio to the political conventions while my hands boxed books and household items.

At the end of August, Mother, Joyce and I returned to the Bay Area. Dick Beard, Vivian's Williams' son, invited us to the Beard family ranch in the Sierras. I went horseback riding with Dick one day, and the horse turned and suddenly made for the partially closed barn door. I bent forward to avoid being toppled, but did not escape my knee scraping the half-closed barn entrance. Mother made me mount a horse the next day and ride with

Dick's step-mother, Darlene. Wisely she said, "Pilots who crash make a flight soon afterwards so fear will not grip them later." Good advice, and I did ride then uneventfully, but I've never mounted a horse since!

On August 31, 1948, a *Little Rascal* whom I did not know, Billy "Froggy" Laughlin, died in a motor-scooter accident in the San Gabriel Valley, near Los Angeles. He, with the highly distinctive low and raspy voice, died at the age of sixteen. He was featured in twenty-nine episodes of the *Our Gang* series, beginning in 1940, two years after my last appearance. Among his last films in 1944 were *Dancing Romeo* and *Tale of a Dog*. Unfortunately, over the years, as so often has been the case, imposters, with unusual voices, have posed as "Froggy." One such gentleman, passing himself off as "Froggy," lived in a town close to the one from which I recently moved. This imposter must not have known that he was posing as someone who had been dead for over fifty years! Sadly, Billy Laughlin's demise was an early marker on the long trail of tragedies that befell *Our Gang* graduates!

And another marker on that "trail of tragedies" was the arrest of Scotty Beckett on suspicion of drunk driving. Scotty appeared in fifteen *Our Gang* shorts, as well as eighty-six other films. He was two years older than I, but we both showed up in *Mike Fright*, (1934), and the *Our Gang Follies of 1936*. This first brush with the law only portended others that would occur in 1954 and 1959 for charges of carrying a concealed weapon, and passing a bad check, etc. Twice divorced before he was twenty-nine, his once promising career in films, and even the TV *Space Ranger* series, spiraled ever downwards.

The magical summer of 1948 was over, and I was soon to enter upon one of life's "peak experiences." A speaker at a recent lecture I attended gave a new meaning for the term "Alma Mater," a name I thought to be only an endearment for the college or university one attends. This lecturer referred to "Alma mater" as the "fostering mother" of a young adult's growing potential, cognitive, social and emotional. What can I say of those three years I spent as a student at Berkeley? Perhaps my advisor in graduate school, some twenty years later, summed up the meaning of those years, when he said, "Those were the golden years, weren't they?" Indeed they were, from start to finish, September 1948 to June 1951! And I did grow, cognitively, socially and emotionally at my own "Alma Mater!" Yet another "foster mother" to help me reach adulthood!

Especially the first semester! The sale of the Woodland Hills house enabled Mother and Dad to give me one semester of living in an approved boarding house "on campus," Arch Place. Thus, for one semester, that important first semester, I had roommates and housemates and the routine of classes and studying, all close at hand. It was the perfect way to start college life!

Berkeley had sent athletes to the 1948 Summer Olympics, held in London, England, that year. The rowing crew had brought home "gold" as well as a diving/swimming champion or two. The University honored its medal winners at the campus Greek Theater soon after classes began. It was a heady time to be at "Cal."!

The University of California at Berkeley is today, as then, one of the great national and international universities. To have studied there for six semesters, under outstanding professors, remains a highlight of my life. With all the Nobel laureates, one felt as if one were at the "hub of the universe" of higher education!

Beyond the academic teaching superiority I experienced, the three fall semesters in which I was enrolled, "Cal" won the P.A.C.-10 first place standing in football. Thus it represented the Pacific coast schools for three years in a row at the annual Rose Bowl Game, — 1948, 1949 and 1950. That meant three trips to Pasadena for me. Who could ask for more?

After the one semester at Arch Place, I had to find a lodging where I could work for board and room. I was a member of the Christian Science College Organization. That group pointed me to a family in need of a live-in babysitter. I lived with the Dr. John Givens family from February 1949 to January of 1950, in their home high atop the Berkeley Hills. Then summer of 1949, I accompanied the Givenses to their American River summer lodge to care for the three children, Judith, Peter and David.

Once, when I was bathing five-year-old David, I was kneeling by the tub. He looked at me in my sweater, and said, "I think you have a bosom!" I smiled to myself, thinking obviously that even five-year-olds, as well as fourth grade nine-year-olds, notice womanly "bumps"! Apparently that's a male awareness, "from the cradle to the grave," my husband observes.

English was my major and Spanish my minor. I read and wrote to my heart's content. Required papers were an exhilarating challenge, and never a struggle to produce. Perhaps my favorite course was the yearlong study of The Great Books, taught by a dashing young professor, Dr. Sears R. Jayne. Office hours with Dr. Jayne were never intimidating, but exciting ventures into further literary learning!

During the year with the Givens family, I made my first acquaintance, in depth, with someone of black ancestry. True, I had known "Buckwheat" in the days of filming the *Little Rascals*, but that had been a very casual encounter. "Susie" was the Givens' maid and cook. We became "buddies," and I visited her Berkeley home. As children, she and her brother had been orphaned on an island in an early twentieth-century hurricane off the Louisiana coast. A Jewish pharmacist and his wife raised the pair as their own children. Susie introduced me to Black-American cooking and culture, thus paving the way to my adoption of two black babies twenty years later.

While I lived with the Givens in the East Bay, I heard that Harpo Marx was giving a concert at the Oakland Civic Auditorium. Mother and I bought tickets. His miming was as delightful as I remembered it, and his harp solos beautiful to hear. I sent a note backstage, as I had done a few years before in Los Angeles, when Chico had appeared solo. Harpo had the usher ask Mother and me to come and see him after the performance. We joined him, minus his curly wig and trademark raincoat. He spoke warmly of Daddy Max and Mommie Winslow, and especially of the years that the Marx Brothers had lived and worked near the Winslows in New York City.

In late 1949 my brother Chester left to study art in Venice, Italy, accessing the wonderful post-War G.I. Bill of Rights for his further education. Chet gave Dad his 1949 Hudson before he left, and I saw my Dad drive a car for the first time in seven years. One trip we took by car that year was to Anderson, California. There I met the Williams aunts and uncles, with whom Dad had only recently reconnected after seventeen years. One of Dad's brothers sold him a small acreage along the Sacramento River. Twelve of Mother's and Dad's final years would be spent at that riverside location, in a home Dad had built for Mother in 1966.

Then it was spring semester, 1950. I left the Givens' babysitting position, needing to earn more than board and room and carfare to "Cal." I decided I would try living at home in San Francisco, and commute to Berkeley. If I scheduled my classes to fall on Mondays, Wednesdays and Fridays, then I could work, baby-sitting at Park Merced, a huge middle-to-upper-class housing project near my home. The housing complex was full of young families with baby-boomers for me to care for on Tuesdays, Thursdays and Saturdays. Even at fifty or seventy-five-cents an hour, the going rate at the time, I could earn the munificent sum of fifty to a hundred dollars a month, more than enough to pay for my commuter fares and for the many books I needed for my English major.

I had dated extensively that first year and a half at Berkeley, living on or near campus and meeting every manner of young man, — an Iraqi foreign student, ex-GIs studying at Cal on the G.I. Bill, and new friends and former classmates from Lincoln High. I put to great use the formals Aunt Grace Kahn and Aunt Rose Cohn had given me. But all that ceased when I moved home. What young man would now travel from the East Bay over to San Francisco for a date? Besides, I needed to work Saturday nights especially, for from that babysitting, I earned the greatest amount of money to pay for school.

What little time I had for leisure or companionship, I turned to a Jewish young man I'd known in the Lincoln High debate club. His family was not rich, but very "comfortable," and there was tremendous love and warmth in their household. I took an instant liking to the young man's mother and she to me, calling me her "shikseleh." (A Yiddish word for a young gentile woman.) The young man and I shared a love of classical music. He taught me to drive his Model B Ford, the first time I went behind an automobile wheel. I so wanted to be a part of that family. Our friendship suddenly turned very serious. My Mother found out that my boyfriend and I were planning to elope to Reno to be married. I never learned how. Perhaps my boyfriend's mother wisely told my Mother.

Shortly before the planned trip to Reno, I returned home from a date, and as I opened the front door, my Mother stood there announcing sternly that the following day I would be flying to Burbank to spend the next two weeks with Mommie Winslow in Hollywood. To my Mother's credit, she must have recognized that she could not relate to me and did not know how to deter my planned escape, but that Mommie Winslow would lovingly open my eyes to the foolishness of an elopement mid-way through University. Frankly, I was relieved, because, deep down I really didn't want to marry that young man; I just wanted to be a part of his loving family. Dad and Mother drove me to the Oakland Airport the next day for what would be my first plane trip. It lasted one hour, then Mommie Winslow and Jack met me at the bottom of the stairs on the tarmac. I spent fourteen tranquil days at the Chateau, encircled by Mommie Winslow's all-embracing love and understanding.

Mommie Winslow also distracted me by asking me to read a new book she had just bought, one she thought a college student should know about and attempt to understand. The book was author Lincoln Barnett's *The Universe and Dr. Einstein*, still considered a classic and masterful exposition of difficult scientific theory.

I told Mommie Winslow that I feared that I would never "hear the end of it," when I returned to live with my parents. I was eighteen now, soon to turn nineteen, and until the current semester, I had lived for a year and a half away from home, and away from my mother's tirades. Mommie Winslow sat down at her dressing table, and wrote a masterful letter to my Mother, which she read to me. In the letter, she more or less put my Mother on her honor not to verbally abuse me upon my return to San Francisco. It was the first time I had ever told Mommie Winslow how cruel and unforgiving my Mother could be.

I returned home and Mother said nary a word about the ill-fated romance. Afterwards, she and I had to spend weekends apartment hunting because, at long last, the city building department had condemned the house we had occupied for almost four years, and we had sixty days to move elsewhere.

It paid to be Welsh and carry the name of Williams, for we found a top-floor, three bedroom, light and airy apartment in the Haight-Ashbury district of San Francisco. Our new landlady, eighty years old, and very alert, was originally from Wales, and her maiden name had been Williams. She liked the look of the four of us and made us welcome.

Just before we were to move from Vernon Street to our new location, my Mother's brother, Uncle Chester, arrived on our doorstep. He was a former editor of a Portland newspaper who had fallen on hard times and turned to alcohol. But in May 1950 he had found work in San Francisco and wished to stay with us temporarily. I opened the door, to hear him exclaim, "My God, you are Julia. You look just like her!" He was referring to his and my Mother's older sister, who had lived on the East Coast for many years. Years later, when I was going through therapy, seeking to understand my Mother's antipathy for me, I would remember this encounter with my Uncle.

It seems my Mother disliked her older sister from the very start, so said my Aunt Julia in my one and only meeting with her in 1966. Somehow, I guess, being the oldest girl in my family, and very much of a temperament and looks akin to my Aunt Julia's, I must have come to embody all the aspects of the sister my Mother could not abide. I enjoyed Uncle Chet's brief stay with us, both in the old and the newer living quarters. He was a tease and a great raconteur. Always I have been grateful he provided a possible, even probable key to understanding my mother's relationship with me!

Whereas 76 Vernon Street had a rent of eighteen dollars a month, 155 Clifford Terrace cost the princely sum of one hundred dollars a month rent. Even though Dad was still not cleared to return to work, Mother had, for a year and a half, been teaching court reporting, again in San Francisco, and the family could afford the more expensive living quarters. That summer of 1950, Dad finally won a small monetary settlement for his industrial accident claim. My parents purchased a carpet, a Kroehler sofa, and a brand new device called a television set. My task that summer was to care for the apartment, shop for, plan and prepare the meals. Dad helped me with the laundry between his job-hunting expeditions. He was fifty-eight, and knew he could not manage hard labor again.

Toward the end of the summer I began a three-days-a-week babysitting job for a family named Williams that lived in an exclusive San Francisco neighborhood. Their neighbors across the street were the Ghiradellis of chocolate fame. My employers were the owners of the Edwards Wire Rope Company, and they moved among the San Francisco social elite of 1950. On the days when I worked, my chief function was to take the children to the nearby park playground for a morning or an afternoon and supervise them there. I thought it hilarious that those whom I saw there with me, also supervising, were young San Francisco society matrons, with their children, and they all seemed to dress uniformly, if still somewhat stylishly. The socialites' habitual garb consisted of tailored white shirtmaker blouses topping black velvet Bermuda-length shorts. Not one of them ever broke ranks with that shared fashion statement. I suddenly realized the wisdom of Mommie Winslow's advice on how to dress. I only remember these socialite ladies fifty years later because they were such slaves to the fashion of the day.

The fifteen months I was yet to stay with my parents, to complete my third year of University, proved to be rather tranquil. With babysitting money I bought my own tickets to plays and road shows of Broadway productions, namely *South Pacific*, *Carousel*, and *Annie, Get Your Gun*, an Irving Berlin musical. Where once, during high school days, I had ushered on Saturday afternoons, I now sat in a balcony seat I paid for myself.

When I went to Southern California for the last of three Rose Bowl games I attended, I stayed with Mommie Winslow the night before my return to Berkeley. Mommie Winslow accompanied me to the Glendale train station early the next morning. We stood shivering in the morning cold waiting for the Daylighter that would take me north. As we thanked each other for the gifts that we had exchanged that Christmas season, we rejoiced about all the "heart-to-heart" talks we had crammed into just a couple of days. "But the greatest gift of all, Laura June, *is what we are for each other*. We have such a great good love between us," Mommie Winslow said, and squeezed my hand. I mounted the steps to the train, smiling, but also crying "tears of joy." She had delivered to my nineteen-year-old heart, for a lifetime's safekeeping, the real meaning of Christmas, — "what we are for each other!"

Shortly after my return from Los Angeles, I would hear from my oldest friend, Roslyn. She had met and become engaged to a fine young man, an accountant and singer of some note. They were to be married toward the end of February in a small Los Angeles ceremony. Then the phone rang a few days after the wedding, and Roslyn announced that she and her new husband Jerry were in San Francisco at the Mark Hopkins Hotel, on their honeymoon trip. Would I come and have a drink with them at the Top of the Mark? Would I! I dressed to the nines in a suit and furs, and though I never drank alcohol in those days, I sipped a ginger ale, and felt very special to be with them on such an occasion.

My favorite beau was Sylvan Kline, a friend from Spanish classes at Lincoln High. We had some wonderful dates that junior year of university, even though we attended rival schools. Sylvan was at Stanford, while I was at "Cal." One evening especially, I silently thanked Aunt Grace Kahn for gifting me with the black strapless gown that dazzled my date at his Stanford formal.

That interlude of romance might have deepened and extended itself the following year had my senior advisor at "Cal" not insisted that I transfer, in my senior year, to the University of California at Los Angeles, the sister school commonly known as U.C.L.A. There he felt I should undertake teacher training to become a Kindergarten-Primary teacher. Though I had almost straight A's in my English major courses, and had wanted to teach high school English, my venerable faculty advisor said, "My dear, you're almost twenty and you look fourteen! You just cannot walk into a high school English class a year from now, and be taken seriously!" Remember, this occurred a decade and a half before the days of "Women's Liberation" from sexual stereotyping!

I spent one final summer in "The City," that "Baghdad-by-the-Bay," as famous columnist Herb Caen termed it. My summer job was waitressing at the Christian Science Benevolent Association Sanatorium in the West Portal district. The facility was French chateau style and very impressive. The interior was flawlessly appointed, and much like my beloved Chateau Elysee in Hollywood. There I was to learn dining room serving skills that would have allowed me to serve meals in any of the world's five-star hotels. Occasionally I served as Captain of the dining room staff, and late in the summer was given charge of a small private dining room for the ill and physically handicapped residents.

Dad was thrilled that I gained such a marketable skill. One day that summer, he said, very wisely, and with some foresight, "When you get married sometime down the road, it may not work out. You better have a skill beyond teaching to tide you over. Be able to do two or three jobs well, then you won't be dependent on any man for the rest of your life!" How well I would remember his advice eleven years later!

CHAPTER 5

WOMANHOOD, WORK AND A WEDDING
1951-54

Home again in Hollywood! In the intervening years, since I last lived there, that little city had changed as much as I had! The influx of military personnel during World War II had changed the patina, and the very core of the environment in which I had reached my teenage years. Now Hollywood, and the boulevard named for it, was not anymore typical hometown fare, — stores and banks, theaters and businesses, — no, now it all became a big tourist attraction! One began to see "souvenir shops," by the dozens. The mass migration to Southern California had begun, and so, once empty fields, — whether in the San Fernando Valley, or the Baldwin Hills, or the San Gabriel Valley, — were now filling up with newly constructed houses. The major movie studios that had ruled the film capital during the twenties, thirties and forties, were now in the process of disintegrating, with independent producers and production companies coming to the fore. Television was making major inroads into movie-going, and because of anti-trust rulings, the biggest of movie studios now were disconnected from their vehicles for distribution, their theater chains, i.e., Loew's, Fox, Warner Brothers, Paramount, etc.

I was on my own now, not quite twenty-one, but emancipated nevertheless. Within the next six months, my parents would separate legally after thirty-one years of marriage, and within the year, I would be prepared to begin my teaching career. But first, I had to find a place to stay while completing my last year of university.

During my summer work as a waitress, I met a gracious lady who asked me to call her when I arrived in Hollywood. She had said she would try to find me a room and board situation, where I could lend a hand to some family in return for a place to stay and to eat, while pursuing my final year of studies. During the week in which I registered at U.C.L.A., I stayed with Mommie Winslow, but it wasn't at my beloved Chateau Elysee anymore.

That beautiful building and grounds had been sold to a religious-affiliated retirement complex. The new owners had asked Mommie Winslow to buy her own apartment, an arrangement something on the order of today's condominium ownership. The price tag was much too high. Mommie Winslow had, for five years at that point, still carried the complete responsibility for her cousin Lena's nursing home costs. Nine years after Daddy Max's death, and after eighteen years at the Chateau Elysee, she had to find elsewhere to live.

Aunt Rose came to the rescue. Next to her one-bedroom apartment at the Chateau Marmont, another one-bedroom apartment was being vacated. Tillie could live there, with Aunt Jane, of course, and it was adequate, but crowded. While Mommie Winslow occupied the bedroom that looked out on the Sunset Strip, Aunt Jane slept on a daybed in the dining room. When I was there, as usual, I slept on the couch.

After a flurry of interviews concerning prospective housing situations, I settled upon a live-in cook and cleaner position in the Beverly Hills home of a dentist, his wife, and son, — the Donald Montgomery family on Palm Drive, two blocks south of Sunset Boulevard. I would maintain a rigorous routine for the next four months.

Up at the crack of dawn to prepare the family's breakfast, then tidy up the kitchen, I would walk up to Sunset to catch the westward bus to

U.C.L.A. and Westwood. Classes all day, five days a week! When I returned to Beverly Hills in late afternoon, there was dinner to prepare and serve, then the cleaning of the kitchen afterwards. By the time I returned to the maid's room in which I slept, I was near exhaustion. Many a night I fell asleep trying to read my assignments and keep up with the homework for each class. Saturdays, I thoroughly cleaned the entire Tudor-style house with its three-bedrooms, den, and formal living and dining rooms. Late Saturday afternoons I would do the family's ironing. Needless to say, few were the Saturday night dates that semester! On one occasion, a young Marine recruit, a former friend from El Monte High School days, escorted me to church, then to see *A Streetcar Named Desire*. Once, another young man took me to a Sunday afternoon movie, and once Syl Kline came down from Stanford, inviting me to a post-football game party. I hadn't been free to attend the game itself.

One October night, the Montgomeries had a catered affair in their back garden. Thank goodness, the caterers were looking after all the food preparation and serving. I was enlisted, in black dress and white apron, to open the front door for guests, to take their wraps, and then to direct them to the garden party. Next I was to go up to Mrs. Montgomery's bedroom, with instructions "to watch the fur coats" of the Beverly Hills elite. I not only watched the fur coats, but I tried on each and every one of them, viewing myself in a full-length bedroom mirror. Ah, to sample what it is, to be dressed like someone in the "Social Register!"

Fortunately I had outstanding professors that semester, especially Dr. Lorraine Scherer, who taught an in-depth class on kindergarten-primary "methods." Berkeley's education classes had given me the teaching fundamentals. Now U.C.L.A. faculty filled in the blanks, as I studied young children's conceptualization, and the deeper aspects of their growth and development. Jeanne Cagney, sister of James Cagney, was a fellow student in my music education course.

Sometimes, especially on Friday nights, I would go to the KNX radio studio on the corner of Gower Street and Sunset Boulevard to attend Steve Allen's original late night *Tonight* radio broadcast. Then past midnight, I boarded the last bus going west to the end of the Sunset Strip, just where that famous thoroughfare joined Beverly Hills. A measure of how times have changed, I dared as a twenty-year-old to walk the several blocks from that junction to Palm Drive and the Montgomery's home. That easternmost part of Beverly Hills still had many vacant lots I had to pass with little or no fear about the hour or the neighborhood. Mommie Winslow and I were great fans of Steve Allen, and she thought it was great I could attend the shows in person. She would listen, tucked in bed!

In mid-fall, on a rare weekend visit to El Monte and Lee's and Carl's, over their back-fence, I visited with a school Trustee for the Mountain View School District. He inquired when I would be ready to begin teaching. Two weeks later, I received a phone call from that school district's Superintendent, Charles Kranz. He had previously worked with Dr. Scherer in the County Schools Office, and admired her teacher training. He asked if I could come for an interview. One late November Sunday afternoon, I met him at his La Puente home.

In from tractoring his orange groves, Mr. Kranz greeted me in a sweaty, grime-streaked tee shirt. Could I come to teach a kindergarten class in February? He would be losing a kindergarten teacher then, and would help me obtain an "emergency" teaching credential. I responded, "Yes, oh, yes, I'll come to teach that kindergarten." I knew I could not sustain the work and study treadmill schedule I had been on for the previous three months.

As part of my preparation for obtaining a teaching credential, I had to have a complete physical examination by a physician. I had a cursory "physical" upon entering "Cal," but in all my twenty years, I had never really been seen, for a thorough physical exam by a doctor, prior to this. Carroll Sax's mother, Gertrude, put me in touch with Seymore Cole, M.D., cardiologist. I went to his Beverly Hills office one Saturday morning, where he cleared me to teach in the public schools. Later I would learn that in the mid-nineteen-fifties he was instrumental in promoting heart massage and C.P.R. measures for the Los Angeles area. What he didn't check that day was my immunization status. Up to that time I had only been vaccinated for smallpox upon entering U.C., Berkeley. I was to learn during the next three years that a primary teacher without immunization is liable to "catch" every childhood disease that comes into her classroom via her pupils. And I caught them all!

Thus it was, in February, 1952, I returned to board and room with my first set of foster parents, Lee and Carl Ingram, that dear couple who had taken me into their home and their hearts as a toddler, almost twenty years before.

Maxson School was just a block distant from the Ingram residence, so I walked to and from work. I had a two-hour lunch break between the two kindergarten classes I taught, and usually spent that time at Gram's. The year I had moved to San Francisco, Gram had sold "the cabin," and moved to another small house on an El Monte half-acre near her daughter Lee's home. Gram, now in her seventies, would serve me lunch and let me nap on one of her beds until it was time for me to return to school for the afternoon session.

Leaving U.C.L.A. in mid-year, I had missed the "practice-teaching" component I should have experienced before I officially entered a classroom. But no matter, there were three generations of schoolteachers before me in my maternal ancestry. I would "swim or sink." I jumped right in with an enthusiasm and love of teaching that saw me through the next three years. Besides taking further classes, in the evenings and summers, to complete my bachelor's degree, I had wonderful fellow teachers who became my mentors, Gloria Hull and Sarah Hill.

Lee and Carl made life pleasant and easy for me. I paid them board and room out of my $280.00 per month salary. Lee was a good cook, and she sewed many of my clothes. I saw Mommie Winslow on the weekends and stayed overnight once each week when I attended a class at the California State College campus, then on North Vermont. "Cal State" had taken over the old U.C.L.A. campus once at that location.

One night at "Cal State," a special speaker was coming to campus, the then famous CBS news analyst, Charles Collingwood. I "cut" my class that night to attend his lecture. Afterwards, I approached the crowd surrounding him, asking him questions. He spied me on the fringes of the group, and reached out to hug me, and said, "What are you doing here?" I talked briefly with him, then turned to leave him with his other admirers. As I left the area, someone asked me, "What did you do to deserve that?" I just smiled, remembering two memorable afternoons almost five years before. Charlie was still as dashing and thoughtful as when we had first met! And my heart fluttered a bit, to be sure!

The Williams family was now scattered. Brother Chester was studying art in Venice, Italy; brother Paul served as an Army cook in Korea; Mother and Dad lived separately; Mother and sister Joyce lived in a house Dad owned in Anderson, California; and Dad, working as a custodian, had bought his own little house on Vicksburg Street in San Francisco. Roger and his growing family were in Santa Monica. Before Chet had left for Europe, he had received first prize in watercolor at the 1951 California Arts and Letters Show.

With Lee and Carl and Gram, I had a close-knit family, with a lot of love and security, close at hand. Perhaps too much, for too long, and for my own good! Looking back, I realize I should have launched off "on my own," getting my own place to live, and learning to drive a car, after I was settled in my teaching position.

I dated some nice young men, but not enough. I even fell in love with one of them. He and I worked together in "little theater" in El Monte. He had studied drama in Hollywood with a Melrose Avenue drama coach. He directed two plays in which I had the lead role. But he wanted bigger things than little theater productions. He was himself an aspiring actor and star-struck, besides.

Laura June Kenny

A publicity shot for a Little Theater production, 1952.

When I thought our relationship was "getting serious," I called Mommie Winslow to see if we might stop by and I could introduce my young man to her. We drove to Hollywood, and parked down the street from the Chateau Marmont. My escort was dazzled when he realized the closeness between Mommie Winslow and myself, and how interconnected her life had been to real "show business" notables. She showed us a photo of a honeymooning Irving and Ellin Berlin, and retold the story of how the Winslows had "stood up" with the Berlins on their long ago wedding day.

The photo of Irving and Ellin Berlin, on their honeymoon.

On the way back to El Monte that night, my thespian friend pleaded with me, every mile of the way, to use what contacts I had, and to urge Mommie Winslow to use her influence, to finally get him his "big break" in show business. Bingo! Déjà vu! I might be used again! I knew that feeling from long ago, — the day of the screen test when I was five. Now again, I wanted what I had always wanted, — a deep, meaningful relationship. I recognized I did not want to be the "means" to another person's "ends!"

I broke off the relationship immediately, and immersed myself in the Christian Science religion. I taught Sunday School, and worked as a member of the local Christian Science Church, alongside Lee and Carl, who were now devout and strictly observant Christian Scientists. Perhaps, I reasoned, I should narrow my focus in boy friends to a choice among the young men of the Christian Science faith whom I knew and had dated.

The summer of 1953, the map I carried in my head suddenly expanded to catalogue the whole United States. I had bought my "hope chest" with some of my first earnings from teaching, but the school year of 1952-53, I saved for a train tour of the nation. It was to be a big, looping trip that would take me more than six weeks and seven thousand miles, renew old acquaintanceships, and give me many vivid memories!

As soon as school was out in June, I left for Detroit, Michigan. There I was enrolled in a two-week advanced course in Christian Science, what Christian Scientists term "class instruction." En route, I spent a few days in "that toddling town, Chicago." I even met a young man, a Christian Scientist, who was my tour guide for those few days.

There were no young men to date in Detroit, but I did tour the Ford Museum complex. However, New York City was another story! There I stayed with a former classmate from U.C., Berkeley, Thelma Norton. My high school and Stanford friend, Sylvan Kline, was now an ensign in the Navy and stationed at Bayonne, New Jersey. We had two wonderful evenings together. He drove me all over Manhattan, pointing out the sights, then we had dinner at a posh restaurant, and saw Rodgers and Hammerstein's, *Me and Juliet*. The final night of my two week stay, Syl and I went for dinner and dancing on the Astor Roof. Who should be across the room at another table, but Aunt Grace Kahn? I didn't tell Sylvan that night, when I took him by the hand to meet Aunt Grace, that it was she who had enabled me to dazzle him with the black strapless dress two years before!

Thelma had a day-job and was studying drama. Almost every night we attended the theater. Old playbills remind me that we saw *Picnic*, *Dial 'M' for Murder*, and *The Seven Year Itch*, as well as some off-Broadway productions. Daytimes I was on my own, exploring the museums, department stores and sight-seeing venues, with only one caution from Thelma, "Don't go down to Greenwich Village by yourself." I obeyed, and instead enjoyed the view from the tops of the Empire State Building and especially the RCA Building. It was unusually clear the day I visited the latter. I could see for a hundred miles in every direction, and experienced a mystical and overwhelming sense of my inter-connectedness to everything I beheld, realizing I was not alone in the universe, and never would be. That comforting awareness has never left me in the fifty plus years since.

While in New York City, I had stopped by the office of Uncle Max Gordon, to say hello, and though he could not get away that day, he called Aunt Millie, and I joined her and her mother Ada for lunch at the Plaza Hotel. Millie Gordon was still as beautiful as ever I remembered her, and Max as preoccupied with show business concerns.

I left New York City for Boston, making a quick pilgrimage there to places dear to the hearts of Christian Scientists, and to historic sites like the Bridge at Concord, and Walden Pond. Then I was bound for Washington, D.C., where Lee's cousin Willard Shaffer was Undersecretary of Labor in President Eisenhower's administration. I stayed at his home and he and his wife gave me a two-day deluxe tour of the nation's capitol.

My final stop was New Orleans. I visited the sites in the French Quarter that my brother Chester had painted when he had been stationed during the war at Barksdale Air Force Base. But I was dismayed by the water-fountains with signs posted, that said, "White Only" or "Colored Only!" I longed to return to California where those discriminations were not the order of the day.

When I returned to California, there was a postcard awaiting me from my brother Chet in Europe. He had been spending a few days with Aunt Rose in Cannes, where he was painting her picture. He wanted to know if I could make it "over here, next summer? Am with Rose at the Majestic. What a sweet and good person she is! Write me in Venice as to whether you might be able to make it or not." How different my life might have been had I really stopped to consider, and then to plan such a jaunt to Europe for the following year.

But instead, September 1953 I dated a young man, just my age, and a Christian Scientist I had met nine years before in my Sunday School class and at El Monte High School. We dated briefly as he was in the Marine Corps, and was being deployed to a stint with his military unit in Korea. He began writing me letters, very warm letters, eventually asking me, via mail, to marry him after he would be discharged the next summer.

I looked around. I was twenty-two. All but two of my girl friends were already married, and some even had children. I truly had a fear of being an "old maid," a "spinster schoolteacher," and I wanted to start my own family. I accepted my suitor's proposal, also by mail, and attempted to get to know his family, in his absence, during the next nine months.

When I would spend my one night a week with Mommie Winslow, coming to the Chateau Marmont after evening classes at "Cal State," our late-night conversations ran the gamut from discussing the wedding plans to current events. She and I were part of the twenty million television viewers who watched the famed Army-McCarthy hearings of spring 1954. Once a week from April 22 to June 17, we recalled the dramatic interplay that had unfolded between the Senator from Wisconsin and Joseph Welch. I could never seem to involve Lee and Carl in political discussions, but Mommie Winslow read widely, so we examined political events somewhat as Dad and I had previously. I relished her curiosity and enthusiasm for whatever was happening in our fast-changing world!

My engagement was announced in May of 1954, while my fiancé was still overseas, but due to arrive home in two months. Waiting for his return, and planning the wedding, I spent a blessed six weeks attending summer school at "Cal State" and living with Mommie Winslow at the Chateau Marmont. Those six weeks, the last I would spend under her roof, were wonderful. We walked every evening, all around West Hollywood, if we were not scheduled to attend the Hollywood Bowl or the Greek Theater with Aunt Rose. Occasionally we drove out to Beverly Hills to see some of the other "Aunts."

Aunt Lena Connors had died the winter before, after seven years being disabled and bedfast. Aunt Jane was visiting in Boston for the summer, so I had Mommie Winslow all to myself, and our sharing was very deep. She opened a packet of love-letters Daddy Max had sent her on the rare occasions when they were apart, and asked me to read them. She told me of the one or two serious arguments they had engaged in, and how they resolved the issues of a religious "mixed marriage," and of a fifteen-year age differential. Theirs had been a totally fulfilling marriage for each of them, with no regrets when death parted them.

I plied Mommie Winslow with questions. I hoped to have the kind of marriage she and Daddy Max had known for thirty-five years, but not the stormy marriage my parents had endured, nor even the moderately happy marriage of Lee and Carl.

Husband-to-be arrived home in late July and promptly bought me my engagement ring. We celebrated with a luncheon at Mike Lyman's Grill in downtown Los Angeles. Something about the meal service distressed Mr. Soon-to-be-married, and he verbally lambasted the waiter. I could have slid out of my chair and under the table with embarrassment! I knew right then and there that the marriage was going to be stormy. I really didn't know this man who would be my husband in four-and-a-half weeks. All the way home I had great uneasiness in the pit of my stomach.

But the plain and inexpensive wedding dress had been bought, and was being made more elaborate by Mama Lee, my sister and sister-in-law were sewing their gowns, the church had been booked, and most importantly, two hundred wedding invitations had already been mailed. It was too late, I thought, to change my mind and tell husband-to-be that we weren't "meant for each other," even if we were both Christian Scientists.

Religion is not enough of a common denominator to serve as the basis for marriage. It does provide a common frame of reference, but it does not automatically supply a shared "world view," and a commonality of the values one holds most dear. I would learn this only by trial and error, and after a period of the next eight years.

In August of 1954, my life was a flurry of pre-nuptial events: wedding showers given me by friends and last minute preparations for the "Big Day." One of the loveliest events was a tea hosted by Vivian Williams, my former high school English teacher at El Monte. Mommie Winslow and all my "Aunts" from Hollywood attended. I had saved the huge sum of three hundred dollars, and with two hundred dollars from Mommie Winslow, and seventy-five dollars from Dad, I managed to create a very attractive late August wedding.

Daddy Carl was deeply involved in developing inventions and placing patents on them, thus two years before, he had left the engineering business world and retreated full time to his garage workshop. With no income, money was scarce for the Ingrams during this period. They had refinanced their home to meet expenses. If they could not help me out monetarily, they were generous in providing all the practical things about wedding preparations. Mama Lee obtained and arranged all the flowers. She also drove me to order and pick up things needed for the wedding reception. Finally the Ingrams hosted the wedding rehearsal dinner at their home.

My parents came from their separate homes in Northern California for the occasion. The affair was strained, and a bit awkward, on account of Mother's rampage against Lee and Carl eight years previously, prior to another wedding in the Williams family. All who were present tried not to notice, and, to their great credit, Lee and Carl just ignored whatever iciness invaded that warm August evening.

Even the night before the wedding I still felt that unease that had begun the day my engagement ring was selected. It had only deepened when my groom-to-be and I paid the perfunctory call at the home of the Minister who would perform the ceremony. The Reverend wanted to see us about "pre-marriage counseling." I had chosen the Presbyterian minister who had married Roger and his wife eight years before. He was a gentle, still rather young man. No sooner was the counseling session begun, when Mr. Soon-to-be-married objected to the tone and the personal content of the discussion, touching as it did upon marital relations. My betrothed abruptly cut short the Sunday afternoon session, and we drove home in silence. I did not then understand terms like "aversion to authority figures," so did not identify what I was witnessing.

The "Big Day" arrived, and I moved through it with a great sense of surprising calm. My sister spent the night with me, sharing the twin beds we had slept in eight to ten years previously at Lee's and Carl's. She looked beautiful for the ceremony as did my sister-in-law, and my oldest niece of five years. They wore gowns of green and carried baskets of asters in purple and pink. The men all wore dress suits, and my groom had his brothers as attendants. Roger sang "The Lord's Prayer," and Uncle Gus Kahn's song, "Your Eyes Have Told Me So."

But I had not looked deeply enough into the eyes of the man who was to be my husband. I really did not know him, and I don't think he ever found out who I was. I would remember later what Gram had said many times about her own marriage: "Sometimes, Laura June, you think you know your husband by the end of the first year of marriage, but I'm here to tell you, sometimes you never know who he really is, or how he will behave!"

CHAPTER 6

CHILDREN, CREATIVITY AND A CRUCIBLE
1954-1962

I became pregnant the first week after my wedding, and was besieged with "morning sickness" for the next four months. Not a good way to begin a marriage, for sure! We had a three-day honeymoon in the desert, and returned to make our first home at Gram's little cottage in El Monte. Immediately after the wedding, she had left by train for Iowa, to see family and friends there. She needed someone to look after her sixteen year old cat and little Pomeranian dog. It was a good arrangement, for we had so hurried into the marriage that we had no time nor money to go house-hunting.

Gram's little house had a guest bedroom where, a few weeks into our marriage, we welcomed Thelma Norton and her traveling companion. They came to see Hollywood for the first time. Thelma and I had shared a class and friendship at Berkeley, and she it was who had hosted me the previous year when I visited New York City. I was only too glad to provide a headquarters from which she and her friend could explore Hollywood, as she had so generously provided a base for me in my visit to "The Big Apple."

Mommie Winslow also had left for the East days after our wedding, thus I couldn't take Thelma and her friend to meet her at the Chateau Marmont. Thelma would have loved that, but we did the next best thing we could think of. We planned to have dinner at the Brown Derby, the Hollywood and Vine show business restaurant, so akin to Sardi's in New York City. Thelma and I had gone to Sardi's, late at night, after we saw Broadway shows, during my stay the previous summer. As the four of us were entering the famous Hollywood eatery, who should emerge but Aunt Rose Cohn, and I introduced our guests to her. Aunt Rose followed us into the Derby and hailed the maitre d'. "Their dinner is to be put on my bill," she smiled, kissed me goodbye and disappeared. My guests were impressed!

Gram arrived back in California the first week of November. Two weeks after we were married, husband-number-one switched jobs, from one in distant Downey, to one in nearby Pasadena. The switch also involved a shift change from swing shift to daytime work hours to coincide with my teaching schedule. This meant, after Gram's arrival, that the three of us shared the evening meal together. She was a great cook, and since, right then, I couldn't stand the sight nor smell of food, I was grateful she offered to prepare our shared supper. However, the first time I left the table, fleeing to the bathroom to unload in the toilet what I had just eaten, she gave my husband a withering look, and announced, "I wouldn't do that to a she-dog the first year!" My husband just laughed. Gram knew from experience. She had conceived Lee on her honeymoon!

Lee and Carl were consternated about my becoming pregnant, not because it was unwise to do so very early on in the marriage, but because it wouldn't "look good" in my position as a Christian Science Reader. I had been elected to that three-year position well before my husband-to-be had arrived home from Korea. Nor was my mother-in-law thrilled either, for exactly the same reason. Seeking comforting validation, I wrote to Mommie Winslow who was staying at the Dorset Hotel, the same New York City hotel in which the Max Gordons lived. With relief I received her acknowledgement of the news of my pregnancy. "It will all work out, dear, don't worry, "she reassured me. She and Gram were very supportive all through the pregnancy.

In January of 1955, we moved to a duplex apartment in downtown El Monte, and I took a bus to work, instead of walking around the corner, as I had for the three previous years. Gloria, my teaching partner, had just been married herself in November, and I had been a member of her wedding party. She helped me through the months until my beloved school Superintendent, Charles Kranz, came to me one day and said, "I can't have you falling, chasing after these little ones in first grade. I'm asking you to take a maternity leave of absence as soon as we can get a replacement teacher for you." It was mid-March and I was in my seventh month.

I did not realize that I had been "burning the candle at both ends," but apparently I had, for I could not sleep enough, when finally my daytime hours were free of school teaching. I would get up in the mornings and get my husband off to work, do a few chores around the house, then go back to bed for a morning nap. After lunch, there would be a few more chores, or shopping for a few groceries, then another nap before my breadwinner arrived home from his workday in electronics. When supper was over, it would not be long before I retired for the night. We owned no television but I listened to the radio and classical music for entertainment. On weekends there were visits to the Ingrams and Gram, or to the home of my in-laws. Of course, there was the Sunday reading at Church until just a few weeks before my due date. I had found a fashion-minded dressmaker in Hollywood who made me an expanding formal gown to wear on the platform-pulpit. Afterwards I would discover that some folks at Church had never even guessed I was pregnant.

My baby was a big baby, and though I had paid three or four visits to a medical doctor, who was also a Christian Scientist, he had never measured me nor examined me internally. He also never told me he was scheduled to be out-of-town at the time my baby was due. My sister-in-law had successfully given birth to four children with the help of this physician, and the births had taken place uneventfully at the Griffith Park Maternity Home, a facility especially geared to the birthing needs of Christian Scientists. We planned to use the same venue.

The night of May 24, very late, my water broke. I had studied natural childbirth books, so I was aware of what was happening, and called the maternity home. The nurse in charge said, "Since this is your first baby, maybe you had better come over now and not wait for your contractions to begin. You have about an hour's drive to get here, don't you?"

I responded yes, and since my bag was packed, we headed out for east Hollywood, the area called the Silverlake district, and the original area for the very first movie studios. I was admitted and bid my husband good-bye so he could go to work the following day. I had not yet had contraction number one. Another mother-to-be was in the building and in labor, set to deliver a breech birth. With the delivery of her child, her screams sent chills up my spine, and I dreaded what lay before me. No form of anesthesia was used in the maternity home

I did not go into labor until late afternoon the next day, and the labor proceeded fairly quickly. My husband arrived after work, and was glad to see that, at last, the baby was on its way. Contractions came, ten, then five, then three minutes apart, and the nurses on duty guided me through the hours until mid-night, when all contractions just ceased. An on-call substitute physician was called in and evaluated that I had gone into something called "uterine inertia." My baby was coming face up, and her head was firmly lodged in my pelvic bones.

Maurice V. Sheets, M.D., obstetrician and gynecologist for some of Hollywood's "rich and famous," dressed in a suit, came at one a.m. in the morning. Pulling on sterile gloves, he examined me and announced, "I'm taking you to Hollywood Presbyterian Hospital, not too far from here. You'll be all right. I'm going to do a Cesarean Section to deliver your baby." The maternity home, perched down a hillside slope, had a stairway of steps up to the sidewalk and our car, so my husband picked me up and very gallantly carried me up that flight of stairs. We followed Dr. Sheets' car as he guided us down back streets to the hospital. Upon arrival in the parking lot, the doctor fetched a wheel-chair, seated me in it, and rushed me to the fourth floor of the hospital, calling over his shoulder to my husband, "You go get her admitted."

By this time, I was so tired, I could not remember my name or address. Nurses changed my gown and put me to bed. I woke to hear Dr.

Sheets talking to his associate, Dr. Gordon Newell, saying, "Look, Gordie, she isn't so green now." I had gone into shock. Outside of my earshot, he told my husband, "I'll save one or the other, but I can't save both." Miraculously he did! My beautiful baby girl was born at 11:19 a.m., May 26, 1955. I spent a week in the hospital. As we were checking out, that precious doctor asked us, "Have you kids got enough money to get out of here today?" We did, but Dr. Sheets had to wait fourteen months to be paid in full for the ten hours he had spent at my side that night and morning, and for his life-saving services.

Mommie Winslow came to see me in the hospital, and I sent her down the hall to the nursery to see her first "grandchild." She, who had lost her one and only child in a stillbirth forty years before, rejoiced with me that both the baby and I had survived. Only weeks after the birth, we met for lunch in downtown Los Angeles and went to Barker Brothers where she chose and bought a maple chest of drawers for the baby's room. I couldn't help but remember the Mission bedroom set she had bought me so many years before!

I loved my precious daughter, who smiled at me in the middle of the nights when I would awaken to nurse her. At five months, when I went out of her view, she called "Mama." We had just moved to the new house built for us on a piece of property adjoining Gram's, the land, a wedding gift to us from Gram and the Ingrams. Our new home was just down the block from Lee and Carl's. I was out in the yard with "Grandma Lee," looking at flowers that needed transplanting, when my daughter called for her mother. What a thrill!

My recuperation from the birth was long, and I had bouts of depression for many months afterwards, but they were not the "baby blues" one hears about. Two weeks after my daughter's birth, a letter had arrived from my Mother, living and teaching in the Mammoth Mountain country of eastern California. I cannot forget the look of her handwriting on the page: "I am sorry to hear that you almost died when your baby was born. Your husband called to say you had a difficult delivery, but this is what you deserved, for all that you have done to me over the years." I showed Mama

Lee the letter, and she said, dismissing it, "Your mother doesn't really mean that!" But I knew that, at some level, she really did!

Twenty-three years later, in a completely different tone, Mother would write me, "Sometimes it comes to me, that you don't know what you have meant to me…..Your faithfulness in caring for Joyce…..all the housework you did with no griping or even reminding….You never once complained of spending half a day caring for Dad during those miserable times he was in and out of the hospital…..It would be awful never to have a chance to thank you *all over again*." But really, that was the *first* and *only* time!

I had planned to return to teaching in the fall, but after the life-threatening birth, I thought I might never risk having another baby, so I wanted to enjoy each day with my daughter. I reluctantly tendered my resignation to a very understanding superintendent, who assured me the door would be always open for my return to teaching. And he was true to his word seven years later!

The home we had built was a lovely postwar model home with many amenities like ceramic tile, hardwood floors and casement windows that rolled outwards. It cost us five thousand, five hundred dollars to build that house in 1955. Gram helped me prune an ancient 'Talisman' climbing rose bush on the property, and the following spring it yielded armloads of long-stem roses, almost too magnificent for any florist shop.

Gram was a wonderful help with my daughter, whom I had named for her, using a European version of her name that was the title of a charming film my husband and I had seen in our dating days. She was thrilled she had a namesake. My little one found it difficult to let go of wakefulness and fall asleep easily. Gram and I would get together evenings as my husband was working swing shift again, and while I ironed clothes, Gram gently bounced my daughter on her knees until the baby fell asleep. "Giggling," she called it.

The fall of 1956, I noticed that Gram was losing weight. The previous spring she had wanted her house to be spruced up with paint. When the days lengthened, Gram and the baby stayed in the yard or on the breezeway while I rolled a fresh coat of paint on her kitchen and living room walls. She had been so wonderful to me through all the years, so full of unconditional love, I wanted to do whatever I could to make her last years bright and beautiful.

I didn't want my first-born to have what I call "the only child syndrome," so I began to do baby-sitting for a local Congressman's district administrator. Our toddlers were only weeks apart in age, and so enjoyed each other's company, just as once Roslyn and I had, at the very same age.

Christmas of 1956 I began foster care of babies abandoned in Los Angeles County. I was one of two or three foster-mothers who would take newborns and young babies left on the steps of churches or in the back rows of movie theaters. In those days there weren't news stories of babies abandoned in plastic bags and placed in dumpsters. Those, who abandoned the babies I cared for, had wanted them to live, and to be found, afterwards, to be looked after. Three "John Does" and one "Jane Doe" and half-a-dozen named babies would come into my care over the next thirty-one months. One little girl, whom we named Beatrice, lived with us for eighteen months. She was the child of a brother and sister, and was awaiting adoption. Eventually, a loving adoptive family was found for her. Expectedly, I cried as the social worker came for her and took her to her new family.

My experience of caring for other children, especially newborns, lessened my fear of again becoming pregnant and facing a problematic childbirth. I found myself yearning to have another baby. Not surprisingly, when my stint of Readership was over in the local Christian Science church, I ceased using birth control and promptly became pregnant in the fall of 1957.

1957 was the last full year of Gram's life. Over a period of nine months, she went to stay with various friends, all the time getting thinner and thinner. Her colon cancer had returned after twenty-two years, but Lee and Carl, because they were strictly adhering to their Christian Science faith, would not take her to see a doctor. Toward the end, a Christian Science nurse did make regular visits, however. She died in Lee's home on January 8,

1958. Three days before she died, I stopped in to see her, and she asked me to come near her bed. She looked at my pregnant body and announced, "The way you carry that baby, I bet it's a boy." Four months later, her prediction would prove correct!

The first three years of my marriage, I remember my husband taking me to Hollywood to see Mommie Winslow on only two occasions, once during my pregnancy, and once when our daughter was a few months old. Jack would bring Mommie Winslow and Aunt Jane, out to El Monte from Hollywood, as often as he could, perhaps every two months. But it was always toward the middle of the day, just when my husband expected his big noon meal to be served, and his lunchbox to be packed, before he left for his swing shift job at Aerojet. One day he complained bitterly about, "You and your rich Hollywood friends!"

Visiting Mommie Winslow with our new daughter.

My pregnancy would prove a good excuse for me to take the old "Red Cars" into Hollywood to see Dr. Sheets for a pre-natal visit, and also Mommie Winslow. One such meeting with Mommie Winslow took place at the old Knickerbocker Hotel where we had a leisurely lunch together after my doctor appointment. I bade goodbye to her on Hollywood Boulevard, she departing westward to her huge apartment on North Crescent Heights, and I heading eastward for downtown, and El Monte beyond. No sooner was I downtown than the afternoon papers blared the headline, "HARRY COHN DEAD." I used a pay phone to call Mommie Winslow's and Aunt Jane answered: "Tillie's not here, Laura June. Aunt Rose had a sudden attack when she heard about Harry dying. Tillie is with her now. I'll tell her you called."

Dear Aunt Rose! She was so the embodiment of the "lady with a lamp," the logo for Columbia Pictures, Harry Cohn's studio. Aunt Rose had "carried the torch" for Harry all those sixteen and a half years since their divorce and his remarriage. Once or twice she had suitors during those years, but she never married. He called her every day and gave her financial counsel, and she always had his picture in her bedroom. The finality of Harry Cohn's death marked the real end of their thirty-five year relationship, and the light seemed to go out of Rose's life. She would be ill with heart trouble for the next twenty-eight months until her death in June of 1960.

A remarkable relationship, it was, between Aunt Rose and my once "Uncle Harry" Cohn. I stopped calling him that when Aunt Rose had divorced him in 1941. Through the years, many times, I had entered her bedroom, and come upon her, seated on the chaise lounge, talking to her former husband, saying, "Yes, Harry, I know. Thanks, I'll do that." However gruff and coarse he was to countless Hollywood folks, he retained a kind of respect and brotherly friendship for Rose. Only two pictures were on Aunt Rose's blonde baby grand piano, a lovely photographic portrait of her niece, Leonore, and a photo of Harry and Joan Cohn's two sons in their military school uniforms. And, not too long after Harry Cohn died, Jack drove Tillie and a recovering Rose out to the Cohn home in Beverly Hills to meet with the widowed Joan. As for Aunt Rose, she never wanted for anything, all her days, courtesy of the Harry Cohn Trust.

It was Harry Cohn who had most certainly installed a young Italian man, named "Johnny N.," to hang around Aunt Rose, serving as her driver, her escort, and most probably her body-guard, all through the early 1950s. Johnny would drive us to the Hollywood Bowl and the Greek Theater, and always join us for the performance. He is seen in one of my 1954 wedding photos in the reception line, just behind Aunt Rose and Mommie Winslow.

Later, when my brother Roger was singing lead rolls in opera for the Santa Monica Civic Opera Association, Johnny would drive Tillie, Jane and Rose to performances of *Carmen* and *Othello*.

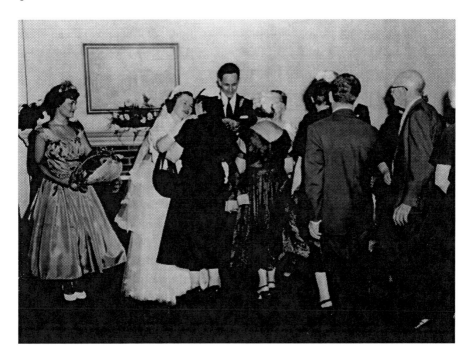

The wedding reception line, with my sister Joyce to my left, Mommie
Winslow embracing me, Aunt Rose and Johnny N. next in line.

Johnny was a pleasant enough fellow, but somehow didn't fit in Aunt Rose's patron-of-the-arts circle. He seldom spoke up, but when he did, it was to make plain to Aunt Rose that whatever she proposed to do was not such a "wise idea" at the time. I thought him a bit bossy, and it puzzled me. Later I was to learn that Harry Cohn had a serious "falling out" with his long time crony, the mobster Johnny Rosselli, the Hollywood point-man for the Chicago "Outfit."

Gangland's Rosselli had come to the movie-capital in the early thirties and connected with most, if not all, studio-heads for the purposes of extortion. The movie moguls' penchant for gambling provided the means for him to exert control over their lives, and their studios' fortunes. He had

165

---

served time in prison following the *Brown-Bioff* scandal. After release from prison, he asked his pal Cohn for a job, but his old friend refused, fearing Columbia stock would sink in value if their names were connected in any manner. Cohn feared retaliation from his one-time friend, and needed to protect not only his present family, but also, even his first wife, the wife whose quarter-million dollar divorce settlement from her first marriage had bankrolled Columbia Pictures, back in January 1924. After Cohn's death, Johnny N. was no longer a fixture in Aunt Rose's life.

Columbia Pictures may well have been named thus because of the ultimate source of the $250,000 Aunt Rose gave Harry to pour into the former CBC (Cohn-Brandt-Cohn) Film Sales. When she was the young actress, Rose Barker, she had met Harry through her brother-in-law, Max Winslow, as the young Cohn was briefly a song-plugger for Waterson, Berlin & Snyder, Daddy Max's firm. They had a short romance, but Harry was soon off to the Army, and the lure of adventure and fortune, through the new-fangled movie business. Meanwhile, Aunt Rose married one of the most important lawyers in both national and New York history, William Nelson Cromwell, of Sullivan & Cromwell. Thirty-five years separated their ages. Cromwell had helped arrange financing of the Panama Canal, after assisting the new entity of Panama to break away from the country of Columbia. Cromwell also helped in establishing the United States Steel Company, and wrote the "Cromwell Plan," the precursor to Chapter 11 bankruptcy protocols. In the process, he became fabulously rich, and Aunt Rose, his young bride, felt like she was a kind of a "Bird in a Gilded Cage."

The May-December marriage did not last for a number of reasons. Rose found her husband's friends, like the father-son duo of J. Pierpont Morgan, too old-fashioned and highbrow. She still liked to take a turn at roller-skating, and her husband looked down upon such practices as undignified and unbecoming for her newfound station in society. For his part, the "Old man Cromwell," Mommie Winslow once told me, "went about the house winding up his collection of clocks." Aunt Rose became bored. She took a trip to California, and saw her old flame, Harry Cohn, who wined and dined her, and danced his way back into her life. Scandal ensued, and made the front pages of the New York papers. Divorce followed, and the hefty settlement from the aging husband came to Aunt Rose. The nation of

Columbia had certainly figured in the fame and fortune of lawyer Cromwell, so it is not surprising that the new movie production firm somehow had bestowed upon it the name of the ancient source of its seed money.

Laura June Kenny

Our second child, a son, was born May 22, 1958. We named him for his paternal grandfather, a Southern gentleman of great warmth and graciousness. The night after the baby arrived, again by C-section, my baby boy's father brought the proud grandfather to my hospital bedside. He looked at me with such joy and gratitude, and said, "Oh, thank you, June darlin'! You have made me so happy!" I adored my father-in-law, and have always rejoiced my older son bears his name.

With both a daughter and a son, I felt so complete. The urge to create anew now manifested itself in my wanting to write, an urge I hadn't responded to since university days. Mommie Winslow gave me her portable Smith-Corona typewriter. My former partner in reading at the church told me of an exciting program of re-orienting and redirecting executives who, for whatever reasons, had lost their jobs. I began writing a series of articles about the program that I envisioned submitting to the *Christian Science Monitor*, that very fine newspaper then and now. Daddy Carl took me to the beautiful old Richfield Oil Building in downtown Los Angeles where we met with the founders of the counseling program. I wrote and submitted the articles, but the *Monitor's* editors were not impressed.

Sometime in 1957 or 1958, my Mother moved back to San Francisco and boarded with my Dad. They lived in the same house, but pursued different interests. She was earning her degree in education so that she could be fully credentialed as a teacher. Practice teaching assignments in "tough" neighborhoods proved too daunting, and she never quite completed her degree. Trips away from El Monte were rare, but once we visited my parents in San Francisco, and Dad treated us to a sixteen-inning Giants' baseball game, while Mother offered to baby-sit the two little ones.

I missed Gram's presence next door. Her little cottage stood dark and empty for many months. Like so many who have cared for an ailing parent until death, Lee felt very bereft when Gram had died the previous winter. The attention she had, at last, showered on her mother, at the end of her life, appeared now to have no other outlet but toward me and my family. Her interest in the day-to-day details of my household became suffocating, and I spoke to Daddy Carl about it one night when he came to repair a washer in one of my faucets. "Daddy, please, Mama Lee calls me all day

Stunning Rose Cohn, smiling in happier days.

long, and always wants to know what I am doing and who is visiting me. Her curiosity is driving me crazy," I pleaded. He assured me he was trying to redirect Lee's interests and energies toward supporting the establishment of thrift stores to benefit a retirement community for Christian Scientists.

About the time I discovered a new life was growing inside of me again, I heard of the death of one who had figured prominently in my brief movie career, Carl "Alfalfa" Switzer. The little boy I had "sighed" over so visibly in *Our Gang Follies of 1938*, had grown to be a man of ill fortune. "Alfalfa" did work in forty-six movies after he completed seventy-two "Little Rascals" episodes, but his parts were not prominent roles but rather, mostly "bit parts." He, like so many other *Our Gang* members, became a washed-up, "has been" child actor, a fate he found difficult to swallow. He tried his hand as a fishing and hunting guide in Northern California, and at tending bar. He was shot and wounded in 1958, and finally died in the San Fernando Valley from a shooting in late January 1959, after a dispute over a fifty-dollar debt. I only remember standing in my kitchen, shocked to hear on the morning radio news of the death of that thirty-one-year-old former "child star." No one had yet breathed the words, "The Curse of the Little Rascals!"

Through all the years, up to this time, I had rejoiced that my two foster mothers respected each other and the contributions they had each made toward my life. They seldom saw each other, but on the occasions when they were together, or when they talked on the phone, their relationship seemed marked by harmony and a shared concern over my well being. Then too, now that Lee and Carl had become Christian Scientists, it appeared that they would share even more in common. Alas, the day before my second daughter was born, jealousy reared its ugly head!

I had taken the two little ones for a long walk, needing to go to the bank to cash a check to cover hospital expenses. I was receiving a cash settlement on a life insurance policy I had taken out on myself in my teaching days. I needed the money to replace savings my husband had used to buy a motorcycle. Lee was driving by and stopped to give us a lift home. She was, as always, unhappy that I was resorting to another C-section for the birth of my third child, insisting that I should trust that Christian Science would take care of everything. Then she asked why I did not call her every day. I responded that my days were full, just caring for my two robust little

Grandpa Carl and Grandma Lee holding our son and daughter.

ones, and getting ready for the new baby. Perhaps I should not have said it, but I added, "I do not call Mommie Winslow very often, but she knows that I love her anyway!"

At this, Lee retorted, "Oh, her! All Mommie Winslow has ever given you is money!" Little did she know! I got out of the car at my front gate with the children, in a state of shock and dismay, and I did not sleep all that night before my baby's birth.

Unhappiness over Lee's hovering over my daily life, plus the advent of that precious second baby daughter in the summer of 1959, — these elements caused us to hunt for a larger home some distance from Elliott Avenue in El Monte. My husband and I found a charming 1924 "picturesque cottage" style house on a large lot in central Arcadia. He had not used his Cal-Vet loan privilege after discharge from the Marine Corps, so that option enabled us to easily purchase the home at 72 West Norman Avenue. The house and bountiful yard, with even a gazebo for the children's playhouse, proved a pleasant setting for child-rearing and exercising creative energies. I braided rugs, baked bread, canned marmalade and pickles, gardened a bit, and wrote every chance I had: letters to politicians, church by-laws, and even a "testimony" for the Christian Science periodicals.

Six years into our marriage, my husband tired of driving me to the store, or much of anyplace else, for that matter, so he ordered me, "Get Lee to show you how to drive." Patiently she taught me the fundamentals, and though it took three tries to pass the driving test in Pasadena, I was finally the proud owner of a driver's license. I loved the freedom driving gave me, and one of the first places I exercised that freedom was to go by bus to Hollywood, and there drive Mommie Winslow's car wherever she wanted to go. Once I had the audacity to secretly take our family car to Hollywood and see Mommie Winslow, all unbeknownst to my husband. Such furtive visits were hard to schedule with little ones to look after, but usually Grandma Lee was only too happy to give me a day-off, once in awhile. And I got away with it!

June of 1960, I drove to Aunt Rose's funeral at the Wee Kirk O' the Heather in Forest Lawn, and greeted a serene Mommie Winslow, dressed in a light spring dress, and not black, just as she was about to enter the chapel. Not surprisingly, she was at peace about Rose's death. Rose's two year illness had ended, and it was a relief, for Tillie had seldom been far from Rose's bedside. Rose had left the Chateau Marmont some years before and moved to an apartment house adjacent to her sister Tillie's. Mommie Winslow wanted me to take particular note of the blanket of gardenias draped over Aunt Rose's casket. "That is from Leonore, and her husband, Walter Annenberg. They couldn't be here, but you know how Leonore loved her Aunt Rose. Isn't it beautiful, Laura June?" That's right, the "princess" I had so admired as a girl, who had known two failed marriages, had at last found her "prince charming" and happiness in the famous publisher and philanthropist Annenberg.

As if three little children were not enough to engage my time and efforts, I let myself be talked into looking after other people's children, — my husband's brother's daughter, the child of a workmate of his at Aerojet, and the children of two of my friends from church. Some of this child-care was "after-school" care, but still I had to be licensed by the county powers-that-be. My earnings from baby-sitting were not saved but promptly spent, helping to underwrite a correspondence law course in which my husband had enrolled.

Then, sometime in 1960, along with the succession of a series of motorcycles my husband had purchased over the years, there appeared in our daily life, over the next eighteen months, a succession of three "house-guests," invited by my husband, but for whom I carried the major responsibility of cooking, washing and cleaning. My husband had put plumbing in a room attached to the garage, thereby creating a "guest-room" where each of the young men could stay. The older woman taken in was crippled by arthritis, and she occupied a hospital bed in our dining room. At the time, I chalked up all this "hospitality" to the warm-heart and generosity of my husband, and I didn't notice the toll it was taking on me, nor our marriage.

Mid-June of 1960 brought the sad news of the death of Guy Kibbee, Jr., my distant cousin Shirley's young brother, born the same year my brother Dickie had died, and whom Mother cared for the spring of 1941. His father, Uncle Guy, the prolific character actor, had died four years before, having been separated from his wife for over a decade. I called Aunt Brownie to express my condolences, though I had not seen her nor Shirley since the move to San Francisco fourteen years before. She was as warm and loving as ever.

Few, in a space of eight years, were the weekend vacations or even an occasional "date" with my husband. I can count on both hands the movies I attended during that time period. When people refer to "films of the fifties," I claim ignorance, having seen so few of them! My "social life," as I dubbed it, consisted of watching the late Jack Paar on television's *Tonight Show*. I would save all my ironing chores to perform while I watched this engaging host in his late-night talk show. Planned vacations were frequently cut short, right in the middle of them, when my husband would suddenly decide to "head home," answering to what he termed, "My homing instinct." Later, when I was reading widely, while going through therapy, I would learn another name for that instinct: *agoraphobia*.

My younger daughter, even at age two, loved to spend time with me in the kitchen, especially when I was baking cookies or preparing homemade bread. Her brother preferred riding his tricycle up and down the driveway or picking fruit from the lower branches of trees. When their sister went off to first grade, both children missed her terribly and pleaded for other playmates. Fortunately, they found an adorable neighbor by the name of Annette, and she lived just up the street.

The fall of 1961 became the "the beginning of the end." In late September I saw Mommie Winslow and Jack, when they drove out to Arcadia and I made a lunch for them, with Mommie Winslow's favorites, chicken-pot pie and a special fruit cocktail. My older daughter had started grade one and just the two younger children were home. Mommie Winslow never appeared to age through the years, though now she was seventy-two. She looked well, or maybe I didn't notice.

Tillie was planning a trip to New York for later in the fall, now that she had finished settling Aunt Rose's estate. She hadn't been East for seven years. Two plus years of caring for Aunt Rose, then disposing of her affairs after her death, had filled the last three and a half years. Harry Cohn's trust fund now passed to Mommie Winslow. She was anxious to see Millie and Max Gordon, the Irving Berlins and so many friends from those long-ago days in New York City. She told me, "Laura June, it isn't good these days to open the mail and see that another friend has died." Her Southern California friends, Gertrude Sax and Alice Reingold, had also recently died. There was a sense of urgency as we discussed her proposed trip over lunch that day.

Six weeks passed and I didn't hear from Mommie Winslow. I imagined she was making preparations to travel east on the train. It was not unusual for us not to connect by phone or note because she knew I had my hands full. If something was important, either she or I called the other. This mode of contact was much in contrast to what had occurred between Lee and myself even since I had moved from El Monte to Arcadia two years before. Lee phoned me daily, sometimes once, often twice, and I was again finding her calls a nuisance and too intrusive. She inquired about every little detail of my daily life. Somehow she couldn't "let go" of me, allowing me the independence I should have had as I entered my thirties. Perhaps she intuited that I had already begun to read what Christian Scientists refer to as "unauthorized literature," books veering far from the tenets and doctrines of the religion in which I had been raised. Had Mama Lee known, that knowledge would have proved threatening to her, so fanatical was her faith in Christian Science, and her adherence to its edicts.

Thanksgiving approached and Dad came down from San Francisco to spend a few days with my family and me. Mother stayed behind, for she was winding down her work as a teacher of court reporting. Dad had been forced to retire as head-custodian for the office building on Sutter Street owned by Qantas Airlines. When that firm realized he was then sixty-nine and was applying for Social Security, the airline promised Dad a trip for two, by air, around the world, for ten cents on the dollar. It was a "golden handshake" he could not refuse. Mother and Dad were scheduled to leave for four months of travel in early February.

A Thanksgiving card arrived from Mommie Winslow and I knew immediately something was wrong. Her handwriting on the envelope and in the card was not her usual expansive, cursive writing so familiar to me. Instead it was cramped, smallish and crooked. I guessed she was ill. I called the apartment in Hollywood and Aunt Jane answered. "How is Mommie Winslow?" I begged to know. "I know something is wrong. Is she ill?"

Tentatively, Aunt Jane responded, "We didn't want to tell you – it's her heart. She had a little spell in late September." Translated, I knew her response meant Mommie Winslow had suffered a heart attack. I remembered Aunt Rose's long bout with "heart trouble," and that their sister, Aunt Sally, had died at age sixty-nine from a heart attack.

And I hadn't wanted to tell either Mommie Winslow or my Dad that I had my own "little spell" in October. During the summer I had written an article for a Christian Science publication and submitted it to the Boston headquarters of that denomination. In October I received a letter telling me my article had been accepted for publication with some minor revisions required.

I was absolutely thrilled. I would finally make it into print. Nothing I had written since high school days had been published. When my husband returned from work, the day I received the letter of acceptance, I told him excitedly about the prospect of publication. He simply looked at me and said, "You know what you could have been doing when you were writing that article? You could have been darning my socks instead!"

I knew. I knew right then and there that man did not know me, did not know who I was or what I was about. And we had been married for seven years and had three children together.

The next day I put the children down for a nap, and lay on the living room couch for my own rest. When I awoke from a brief sleep, I was lying in a pool of blood. I cleaned up the mess as best I could but told no one that I had hemorrhaged. For eight months afterwards, my menstrual periods would last for at least two weeks or longer.

As soon as Dad left for San Francisco, I asked Grandma Lee to look after the children while I drove into Hollywood twice a week to see Mommie Winslow. Since I had only been driving for just over a year, and had never yet used the freeway system of Los Angeles, I got from Arcadia to Hollywood via back roads through South Pasadena, Eagle Rock and Glendale. The Los Feliz district, east of Western Avenue, was marked by large, sumptuous residences, and yet there remained some open fields of truck gardens with roadside flower-stands. I always stopped, en route, to buy flowers for Mommie Winslow, especially little bunches of violets.

I must have gone to 1360 N. Crescent Heights a half-a-dozen times over the next three weeks. Mommie Winslow would be sitting up in bed, her hair and nails done, and we made "small talk." Once she wanted to have me get her jewelry, locked away in the closet. "I want you to have some things of mine." In that closet was all of Aunt Rose's magnificent jewelry collection as well, including her twenty-five carat diamond ring.

"Oh, no," I said, "Don't bother with that now." Maybe I wanted to forestall the inevitability of her death by not acknowledging its nearness, but at the time, I thought it was inappropriate for her to be giving me her jewelry. I wanted her to be concentrating on recuperating and getting stronger.

One day we sat by the sixth floor bedroom window that looked out over West Hollywood and the Sunset Strip. I was beginning to recognize that probably Mommie Winslow's life was drawing to a close, but I wanted to give her "something to live for" in the future. I began talking of my three children and said, "Darling, don't you want to see how they turn out when they are grown?" She didn't answer but only looked out into the distance and was silent for a long time. Then I knew it was of no use to posit a future for her consideration. Finally, and I now realize I said it intuitively, "Well, you have had such a wonderful, full life, haven't you?"

She turned her gaze and looked back at me with those great big brown eyes and smiled, "Oh, yes. It has been such a good life." That afternoon was the last I was to see Mommie Winslow for five-and-a-half weeks. A day or two after this visit, I rear-ended a car as it was making a slow right turn into a driveway. I had been distracted, by trying to avoid the path of a passing bicyclist. Driving privileges, especially to Hollywood and back, were revoked by my husband forthwith.

Shortly thereafter Mommie Winslow had a second and more severe heart attack and was taken to Cedars of Lebanon Hospital, where Daddy Max had died nearly twenty years before. She begged to come home to her apartment for Christmas, always her favorite time of the year. Her wish was granted, but from then on she had fulltime medical supervision by a registered nurse.

Mid January 1962 I felt impelled to make it to Hollywood, one way or another, to see Mommie Winslow. Aunt Jane suggested that I come and have lunch with her. Grandma Lee agreed to take care of the little ones that day, and drove me to the bus in Arcadia where I started for downtown Los Angeles. From there I would take a second bus out to Hollywood. The trip would take two hours. It was January 18.

My Mommie Winslow had such a changed appearance. She had lost twenty pounds and her hair was now pure white, not the golden brown hair she had always achieved by having it colored for the twenty-seven years that I had known her. We ate lunch together, just the two of us, while the others present, Aunt Jane, Tillie's old friend, Grace Aubinger, and the nurse, ate elsewhere. I asked Mommie Winslow about the proposed trip to New York City or the possible visits to California of friends from there, possibly the Gordons, or the Berlins. She made vague responses and I knew there would be no more trips for her.

About two o'clock, Jack arrived. He had a swing-shift job at one of the film-processing plants in Hollywood, and always kept his afternoons free to take Tillie wherever she wanted or needed to go. That afternoon, he said her afternoon drive would consist of taking me back to Arcadia. We descended in the elevator, wordlessly, but with her hand clinging tightly to my hand. There was no need to talk. We were together. That was all that mattered!

The 1942 Dodge, still in great working order, was maneuvered by Jack down familiar streets eastward: Sunset Boulevard to La Brea Avenue, then north to Jack's old stand-by route, Franklin Avenue, with its ups and downs, then onto the Hollywood Freeway and just past the former Chateau Elysee. "Oh, what a beautiful building!" Tillie exclaimed, as if she had never seen it before. "What is it?" she asked, as we passed her former residence.

"Why, Tillie, you should know! You lived there for 18 years. It's the Chateau Elysee, but they call it by another name now," Aunt Jane explained.

I held Mommie Winslow's hand all the way to Arcadia, she and I in the back seat with the nurse, Aunt Jane, Grace Aubinger and Jack sharing the front seat. Jack soon left the freeway to take the back streets through north Los Angeles toward South Pasadena. We moved down Prospect Avenue with its overhanging trees a panoply of brilliant green. Mommie Winslow loved that street and those trees. Jack had taken that route many times to get to my house.

Finally we reached Arcadia and my home on Norman Avenue. I got out of the car, bent in and hugged and kissed Mommie Winslow, promising, "I'll come soon again. I love you."

"Oh, yes, please do!" she said. Precisely twenty-four hours later the phone rang in my breakfast nook. It was Aunt Jane: "I have some bad news for you. Tillie just passed away before Jack could take her for the afternoon drive."

"Oh, no, I'm so glad I saw her yesterday," I sighed and leaned against the wall. And I felt incredibly grateful I had felt impelled to make the long bus ride the previous day. Providence again, —the law of compensation, — leading the way. I now know from my many years as a palliative care volunteer that, at some level, she had probably waited to make her exit until she had seen me one last time. It was Friday, January 19, 1962.

I was to learn later from Grace Aubinger that Jack had come that Friday, at his usual hour, and they were preparing to take the customary afternoon drive. Tillie had complained of feeling "so cold," so the nurse had brought a fur coat to put about her shoulders. She collapsed at that moment and was gone. And thus, so quickly and so gently, an era ended, for her, and for me, and for all who treasured her friendship. Overwhelming gratitude for those last hours with her overshadowed the grief I would feel, and still feel, for her loss.

The first persons I contacted with the sad news were my parents in San Francisco. Bless Mother's heart! A week later, she wrote me words of great comfort: "Seeing the places you associate with Tillie will hurt for some time, and then you'll find that the things you associate with her will give way to the thoughts you shared together. And then later, when you see a jacaranda tree, you'll remember all Tillie's joy in doing for you and for us all, and the goodness that permeates every memory of her. Then Hollywood, with all its memories, won't hurt you any more, but will bring you a warmth and nearness to her. At least that's what happened with me when Dickie left." And she went on to describe how she had come, eventually and somewhat, to terms with my baby brother Dickie's death.

I also called Grace Kahn right after Aunt Jane's phone call and broke the news to her. Somehow I had to reach out to all those who had been my "Aunts" for all those many years. "It's the end of an era, and sadly so," Aunt Grace sighed. "I will miss her so." That theme was echoed time and again in the messages I received after Mommie Winslow's death.

A letter that really comforted me came from Lucille Capra, in response to one I had written the Capras: "Of course we remember you. Tillie and Max talked so much of what they wanted for you. They had great love for you. Tillie and Max would be very proud of you, I know. We feel they gave us so much. They were true friends and we miss them still."

Lu Capra, fishing, in the days when she and Frank visited the Winslows at their Thousands Islands cottage on the St. Lawrence River.

The Max Gordons could not come out from New York City for her funeral service, but Aunt Millie wrote me a few months later, "Even though I didn't see my dear Tillie very often in the last few years, I miss her very much, and when she left us, we were planning a reunion. Max and I went to California shortly after. Needless to say, I didn't enjoy it very much without her there."

The morning of Mommie Winslow's funeral at Forest Lawn's Wee Kirk O' the Heather Church, I arose before anyone else and wrote Jack a letter, pouring into it all the love and loss I felt for the woman who had been a "second Mother" to both of us. Sitting in the Church that day were Frank and Lu Capra, Aunt Grace Kahn, and many others whose lives Tillie had touched and graced. To honor her, I asked the man who was officiating to read Proverbs 30, the description in the Jewish Bible of "A Woman of Valor." A spray of violets I sent lay next to the orchids Jane had placed on the closed casket. Afterwards when we all drove up the hill to the gated, enclosed Gardens of Memory, I saw Jack up close and fell into his arms, sobbing, pressing that letter into his hands before Tillie's burial.

Sadly, my husband did not believe in post-funeral receptions, nor did he feel affinity for the other mourners that day, so we went straight home after the burial, and not over to the gathering Aunt Jane was having back at 1360 Crescent Heights. I have always regretted that I could not be present with Mommie Winslow's friends, those lovely folks who had peopled my childhood and young adulthood. What wonderful stories I would have heard that day that I might have been able to relay here!

Over the previous seven and half years, I had never discussed with Mommie Winslow my unhappy marriage, my frustration about my writing, nor my being asked to care for three "perfect strangers" in my home. *But I know that somehow she knew.* In an act of ultimate compassion and discerning mother love, I would learn, a month after her death, that she had left me a large monetary bequest from her estate. She had bought and paid for my ticket from a failed marriage, and my ticket to a fulfilling education and career, to creative opportunities, and best of all, to independence and a new life for me, and my children.

It was indeed Mommie Winslow, along with Mama Lee, who had spared me the so-called "Curse of the Little Rascals." *I had fled the fates of fame and celebrity at too young an age, exploitation by hangers-on and even those close to "the star," exposure to the dark underside of movie-making, and most especially, loss of my childhood.* She and Lee, and their husbands, had brought to my childhood, instead, some semblance of normalcy, albeit "not run of the mill" normalcy. And it was Mommie Winslow who had encouraged higher education with expanding horizons and creativity. For twenty years after her death, and all through graduate school, I would write on that portable Smith-Corona she had handed me early in my marriage. "So you can write about all the things we have shared," she had said.

Tillie's death also paved the way for me to leave Christian Science permanently. That well-meaning religion had not saved her life nor spared her death, though aspects of its teachings comforted me in my grief.

With that human "other" gone who so personified "a different way of being," I now had to look to the One who had brought Tillie and all the others into my life, the One I call Providence, that *Law-giver of the law of compensation* and that *Author of human connectedness*. One long, wonderful and exciting movement of the dance of Life was surely over, but the dance prevails. The "lord of the dance" continues with the choreography, and with me. The score for my lifetime plays on, and I dance!

EPILOGUE

"Whatever happened to some of the other Little Rascals?"

Since there were approximately three hundred children who appeared in the *Our Gang Comedies* over the space of twenty-two years, 1922-44, the following, in no way, can be an exhaustive account, nor anyway comprehensive in nature. The author has chosen to name some persons most remembered among the casts, —and there were many such casts over the two plus decades. Many of us, who served as "extras" and "bit players," grew up to fade into obscurity, and then to lead very ordinary lives not connected to show business. We became secretaries, teachers, business men and women, and at least one of us became a physician. For some of us fate was kind. For others, life became a "mixed bag," and then there were those others, whose lives ended sadly or much too soon! Herewith is a *sampling* of "Whatever happened to."

Matthew "Stymie" Beard: Born in 1925, he appeared in three dozen *Our Gang* shorts, then took bit parts in feature length films, eventually dropping out of pictures and high school to lead a life of petty crimes and drugs for twenty-five years. He experienced rehabilitation from the drug scene eventually, and died from pneumonia at age 56.

Scotty Beckett: Born in 1929, he made appearances in seventeen *Our Gang* episodes, then went on to many fairly prominent roles in major films, tried stage productions, was heard as a radio regular, and even starred in an early television series in the 1950s. As early as 1948 he ran afoul of the law, was arrested on many occasions over the next twenty years, toyed with drugs, and died after a beating, and perhaps from a drug overdose, at age 38.

Tommy "Butch" Bond: Born in 1927, he was seen in twenty-seven *Our Gang* films and numerous other films until he enrolled in and was graduated from Los Angeles State College in 1951. Thereafter he began working in Hollywood and elsewhere in the production end of the infant television business, professing to enjoy being "behind the camera," instead of in front of it.

Norman "Chubby" Chaney: Born in 1918, he appeared in eighteen *Our Gang* shorts for a brief two years, then returned to his native Maryland where he underwent an operation for his morbid obesity. He never fully recovered from that surgery, and he died in 1936 at age 18.

Joe Cobb: Born in 1917, he made appearances in a prolific eighty-six *Our Gang* episodes over seven years, as well as a dozen other films. In young manhood he joined the war work force, later serving at a Southern California industry plant for three decades. In 2002, he died of natural causes at age 84.

Jackie Condon: Born in 1918, he was seen in a hefty seventy-eight *Our Gang* films over the span of seven years, then did not find theatrical work thereafter. He died of cancer at age 59.

Jackie Cooper: Born in 1922, this actor appeared in fifteen *Our Gang* shorts over a two-year period, then went on to an illustrious film and television career, acting and directing. Finally he walked away from his life-long show business career in 1989, at age 67.

Mickey Daniels: Born in 1916, he made appearances in forty-nine *Our Gang* episodes during a four-year period, then went on to be seen in fifty other films up through World War II. He left filmmaking to enter the construction business at many sites throughout the world, and had a family, but died alone in a hotel, of cirrhosis of the liver at age 55.

Johnny Downs: Born in 1913, he was seen in twenty-three *Our Gang* films over the span of five years, then went on to be seen in over sixty other films, on stage, and in vaudeville appearances, and even hosted a television show in his later years. He died of cancer at age 80.

Mickey Gubitosi, a.k.a. Robert Blake: Born in 1933, he was brought by his parents to Los Angeles from the East Coast, and in 1938 first appeared in the *Our Gang* series, showing up in forty episodes over five years. He was later seen as a child in the *Red Ryder* westerns, then in several feature films. School attendance was sporadic and he "dropped out" of education, opting to dabble in drugs and alcohol. Known now as Blake, he did a stint in the service from 1954-56, then returned to acting, putting in memorable performances in the film *In Cold Blood* and in the television series *Baretta*, for which he received a 1975 Emmy. There have been other acting performances, but to know his current situation, one has only to read the daily papers or to watch television news shows. Blake has been very vocal about his dysfunctional family as a child and about the difficulties facing child performers.

Robert "Wheezer" Hutchins: Born in 1925, Bobby made fifty-eight appearances in *Our Gang* shorts during a six year span, plus a couple of other film appearances. Little is known of what happened next except that he died just short of his twentieth birthday in a military airplane crash, at Merced, California, while in the service of his country during World War II.

Darla Jean Hood: Born in 1931, precocious Darla was seen in fifty *Our Gang* films over six years. Though she appeared in few films afterwards, she worked on stage, in television, and in nightclubs, and made personal appearances on big-name shows. She had quite a range of vocalization, thus she was asked to do "voice-overs" for movies and commercials. She died of hepatitis in a North Hollywood hospital at age 47.

Allen "Farina" Hoskins: Born in 1920, this child performer took the prize for the most appearances in *Our Gang* episodes, 105 of them during a nine-year period, 1922-1931. He later appeared in a handful of other films, served in World War II in the South Pacific, then dropped out of show business to work in Northern California with the mentally challenged. He died of cancer at age 60.

Eugene "Pineapple" Jackson: Born in 1916, he played the role of "Farina's" older brother in six *Our Gang* episodes over a brief two-year span. He appeared in mostly bit parts in forty-four other films, performed in vaudeville tours, and was seen periodically in television episodes up through 1992. He was proprietor of a dancing school in Compton, California, for many years, and died of a heart attack at age 84.

Mary Ann Jackson: Born in 1923, she showed her freckled face and memorable haircut in thirty-two *Our Gang* films over a period of three years, 1928-31. She also appeared in twenty-five other films prior to her stint with Hal Roach's *Little Rascals.* After leaving *Our Gang,* she made one more film in 1950 and a television appearance in 1964. She lives in Southern California.

Darwood "Waldo" Kaye, a.k.a. Darwood Kenneth Smith: Born in 1930, this bespectacled nerd of a performer, appeared in twenty-one *Our Gang* episodes over four years. There were a few bit parts to follow in other films, then service with the army. His life-work became the ministry and missionary work of the Seventh-Day Adventist Church. He retired to Riverside, California, where, while walking along a sidewalk one day in May 2002, he was killed by a hit-and-run driver, at age 72.

Mary Kornman: Born in 1915, she appeared in forty-one *Our Gang* shorts from 1922-26, then was seen in bit parts in forty-seven undistinguished films until 1940. She died of cancer at age 57.

William "Froggy" Laughlin: Born in 1932, this little boy with the deep, rough voice was seen and heard in twenty-nine *Our Gang* films over a period of four years. He died as the result of a motor scooter accident in La Puente, California, at age 16.

Eugene Gordon "Porky" Lee: Born in 1933, this round-faced charmer made forty-three appearances in *Our Gang* episodes from 1934-1939, then left Hollywood for Texas. Last heard of, he was teaching in Minnesota after a long teaching career.

George "Spanky" McFarland: Born in 1928, this pudgy little fellow was great for close-ups, for he developed unforgettable looks of exasperation. He appeared in nearly a hundred *Our Gang* shorts, over an eleven-year span, as well as a few other feature length films before he left Hollywood for his native Texas and completion of his teenage years. There was a very brief stint in the Air Force, a lot of miscellaneous jobs, mostly sales work, and even a five-year fling with his own television show aimed at the young crowd. Then he worked for several years for the Philco Corporation. He helped to honor his former boss, Hal Roach, at the 56th Annual Academy Awards ceremony in 1984. Nine years later he died of a heart attack in Texas, at age 64.

Dickie Moore: Born in 1925, he had a short one-year contract with *Our Gang*, but managed to appear in eight comedies during that 1932-33 season. Over a thirty-year career from babyhood on, he would show up, with some rather good parts, in ninety-five other films and a few television shows. He gave Shirley Temple her first screen kiss in 1942. Staying connected to show business, he moved to New York and went into public relations. In 1988, he married singer/actress Jane Powell.

Petie, the Pup: Many canines through the years played the part of the dog with the circle around his eye. But one of the first of these pit bulls, who had been appearing for three years in *Our Gang* films, was found dead in 1930, having been poisoned by an unknown person.

Jay R. Smith: Born in 1915, he was a freckled-face youngster who appeared in three dozen *Our Gang* shorts from 1925-1929. Thereafter, he left show business, served in the Army during World War II, owned a paint store, lived in Hawaii, and spent his last years in the Las Vegas area. In October, 2002, his stabbed and mutilated body was found in the desert, twenty-five miles north of the city, a homicide victim of a homeless man whom he had befriended. Smith died at age 87.

Carl "Alfalfa" Switzer: Born in 1927, he and his brother came from Illinois to Los Angeles, where he was seen in sixty-one *Our Gang* episodes over five years years, from 1935-40. As well, over the next eighteen years he appeared in fifty-six other films, and the Roy Rogers television series, though his parts were small in nature. He had to supplement his movie and television jobs with bartending and serving as a hunting and fishing guide to bigger name movie stars. In 1958, we was mysteriously shot and wounded, then shot to death by a former business partner the following year over a gambling debt. The death was termed "justifiable homicide." Alfalfa died at age 31.

Harold Switzer: Born in 1925, he was the better looking of the two brothers, but had to take a backseat to the onstage and offstage antics of his more famous brother, "Alfalfa." He was in twenty-nine *Our Gang* shorts in the period of 1935-40. I stood next to him in the singing finale of *Our Gang Follies of 1938*. Little is known of what Harold did after his tenure with Hal Roach's Rascals, except that at one time he owned and operated a Laundromat. Sadly, in 1967, nine years after his brother's death, Harold killed his girl friend, then committed suicide a few hours later. He died at age 42.

Billie "Buckwheat" Thomas: Born in 1931, this beloved, engaging performer was seen in ninety-three *Our Gang* films from 1934-1944. He made only a few other film appearances, then dropped out of movie-making. He served in the Korean War, and in 1954 became a film lab technician. He died of a heart attack in 1980 at age 49.

Beware: Myriad, through the years, are those persons who have attempted to capitalize on the fame and celebrity of Hal Roach's *Little Rascals* by impersonating many of them, claiming to be "the real thing." Such hoaxes, by fame-seeking imposters, have occurred many times over, and are still taking place. Research in books and on the internet will set any inquirer straight.

Last but not least, there is **Me,** with a pay-stub from the Hal Roach Studio and a social security identification card, indicating that the Hal Roach organization gave me my first job. Read on, to find out a little about *"Whatever happened to the author of this book?"*

Laura June Williams (Kenny): Born in June of 1931, my impoverished parents moved my brothers and me from Washington State to Los Angeles in July of 1932. Economic conditions were no better in sunny California than the great Northwest, and so all four of us were placed in foster care for longer and shorter periods. Reading this book will tell you what happened next. Work in movie studios put food on the family table, so my brothers and I, and later, our younger sister, all appeared in various movies before World War II.

Our family was never the same after that world conflict, and we scattered in different directions. I lived in the San Francisco Bay Area for five eventful postwar years, during which I was privileged to attend the University of California at Berkeley. In 1951, I returned to Los Angeles, attended U.C.L.A., and took a job teaching school. I married in 1954, and had two daughters and a son. I divorced in 1963, resumed teaching and my own education. In 1964 I married a former Canadian, and five years later we adopted a son and a daughter. Our family moved to Canada in 1972. The older children eventually returned to California, but our younger children grew up in Canada, where again I taught school. In the 1990s, all of us returned to the United States.

For twenty years I have volunteered in the field of hospice and palliative care, for two of those years maintaining a web-site addressing end-of-life issues. With my husband, I now live in the San Fernando Valley, and together, we write, educate and speak about death and dying, and work, hands-on, in the field of hospice. In my spare time, I edit memoirs for my friends and am transcribing my pioneer Great-grandmother's 1874-1896 journal. I enjoy gardening, and swim a quarter-mile of laps three times a week.

Whatever happened to some of the cast of characters in my life?

Dad (Russell Williams): Dad lived in Northern California and Idaho until his death from a stroke in 1984, at age 92.

Mother (Hazel Williams): Mother lived also in California and Idaho until her death in 1995, at age 94.

Brother Chester Williams: Lived with his wife in England and painted professionally until his death in 1994, at age 73.

Brother Paul Williams: Lived with his wife in Southern California until his death from cancer in 1996, at age 71.

Daddy Carl Ingram: Lived with his wife Lee in El Monte until his death, from a heart attack, in 1972, at age 67.

Mama Lee Ingram: Lived out her life in El Monte until her death, from a heart attack, in 1975, at age 72. Unfortunately, the Ingrams and I were estranged over the issue of my leaving the Christian Science religion.

Aunt Grace Kahn: Lived in Beverly Hills and corresponded with me until her death in 1983 at age 92.

Aunt Millie Gordon: Lived in New York City, and we corresponded until the death of her husband. I visited the Gordons there in 1973 and we talked by phone in 1977 during the blackout.

Uncle Max Gordon: Lived in New York City and wrote a book about his life in 1963. He died in 1978 at age 86.

Aunt Jane Winslow: Lived in Hollywood until her death in 1968 at age 77. We were close, and I visited her two days before her death.

Mr. and Mrs. Frank Capra: They lived both at Fallbrook and La Quinta, California, in their last years, he writing and lecturing until felled by a stroke after Lu Capra's death in 1984. He and I corresponded until he suffered that stroke in 1985. Frank died in 1991.

Vivian Williams: Her San Dimas home was my headquarters whenever I visited Southern California after moving distant from the Los Angeles area. We wrote and called each other on a regular basis until her last illness in 1995. Our deep friendship spanned fifty-one years. She died in 1996, at age 89.

Jack Calhoun: Jack lived with his wife Pat in Hollywood until his retirement from his film lab work, at which time they moved to the Santa Barbara, then the Monterey area of California. My husband and I visited them at both locations through the years. Jack died in 2001, at the age of 85, at the Motion Picture and Television Fund Home in Woodland Hills. Fortunately, after we returned to California, we were able to be with the Calhouns on a more regular basis. And we treasure our last visit, just weeks before Jack's death.

BIBLIOGRAPHY

Barrett, Mary Ellin. *Irving Berlin: A Daughter's Memoir*. New York: Simon & Schuster, 1994.

Bergreen, Laurence. *As Thousands Cheer: The Life of Irving Berlin*. New York: Viking Penguin, 1990.

Binder, John J. *The Chicago Outfit*. Chicago: Arcadia Publishing, 2003.

Bozer, John Wilson and John Lee Brooks, eds. *The Victorian Age: Prose, Poetry and Drama*. New York: Appleton-Century-Crofts, 1954.

Capra, Frank. *The Name Above the Title: An Autobiography*. New York: The Macmillan Company, 1971.

Chandler, Charlotte. *Hello, I Must Be Going: Groucho and His Friends*. New York: Doubleday & Company, 1979.

Cooney, John. *The Annenbergs*. New York: Simon & Schuster, 1982.

Emerson, Ralph Waldo. *Compensation*. New York: Thomas Y. Crowell and Company.

Gordon, Max with Lewis Funke. *Max Gordon Presents*. New York: Bernard Geis Associates, 1963.

Green, Abel and Joe Laurie Jr. *Show Biz: From Vaude to Video*. New York: Henry Holt and Company, 1951.

Gulick, Rebecca. *Those Little Rascals: The Pictorial History of Our Gang*. Avenel, NJ: Brompton Books Corp., 1993.

Hirschhorn, Clive. *The Columbia Story: The Complete History of the Studio and All Its Films*. New York: Crown Publishers, Inc., 1990.

The Internet Movie Database. URL: www.us.imdb.com.

Jablonski, Edward. *Irving Berlin: American Troubadour*. New York: Henry Holt and Company, 1999.

Kenny, Laura June. "Christmas in Hollywood". *Kingston Whig-Standard Magazine*, (Kingston, ON), December 21, 1991.

___. "His 'Crudeness'—My Complex 'Uncle Harry Cohn.'" *Pahrump Valley Gazette*, (Pahrump, NV), March 1, 2001.

___. "Finder and Promoter of Talent—My Own Daddy Max." *Pahrump Valley Gazette*, (Pahrump, NV), January 25, 2001.

___. "Grandma's Diamonds." *Kingston Whig-Standard*, (Kingston, ON), July 1992.

___. "Max Gordon—from Rags to the Riches of Broadway." *Pahrump Valley Gazette,* (Pahrump, NV), February 8, 2001.

___. "A Prolific Actor and Mother's Cousin—Guy Kibbee." *Pahrump Valley Gazette,* (Pahrump, NV), February 22, 2001.

___. "The Rage and Despair of Inarticulate Youth." *Kingston Whig-Standard*, (Kingston, ON), March 26, 1994.

Laura June Kenny

___. "Remembering Frank Capra." *Kingston Whig-Standard Magazine*, (Kingston, ON), September 21, 1991.

___. "Remembering: Hollywood and Los Angeles When They Were a Paradise!" *Pahrump Valley Gazette*, (Pahrump, NV), January 18, 2001.

___. "Some Say Capracorn—I Say Capra Had Zest For Life!" *Pahrump Valley Gazette*, (Pahrump, NV), February 15, 2001.

___. "Songwriters Gus and Grace Kahn—Their Life a Love-story!" *Pahrump Valley Gazette*, (Pahrump, NV), February 8, 2001.

___. "Summer in Yosemite." *Kingston Whig-Standard*, (Kingston, ON), August 28, 1993.

___. "A Valedictorian's Date with Charles Collingwood." *Kingston Whig-Standard*, (Kingston, ON), July 1993.

Maltin, Leonard and Richard W. Bamm. *Our Gang: The Life and Times of the Little Rascals*. New York: Crown Publishers, Inc., 1977.

Marx, Maxine. *Growing Up With Chico*. Englewood Cliffs, NJ: Prentice-Hall, Inc, 1980.

McBride, Joseph. *Frank Capra: The Catastrophe of Success*. New York: St. Martin's Griffen, 1992.

McGuire, Frieda K. "June's Essay on Teachers." San Francisco: *Sierra Educational News*, California Teachers Association, June 1944.

Moore, Grace. *You're Only Human Once*. Garden City, NY: Doubleday, Doran & Co., 1944.

Stoddardt, Dayton. *Lord Broadway: Variety's "Sime."* New York: Wilfred Funk, Inc., 1941.

St. Johns, Adela Rogers. *The Honeycomb*. Garden City, New York: Doubleday & Company, Inc., 1969.

Thomas, Bob. *King Cohn: The Life and Times of Harry Cohn*. New York: G. P. Putnam's Sons, 1967.

Tucker, Sophie. *Some of These Days*: *The Autobiography of Sophie Tucker*. Garden City, NY: Garden City Publishing Co., Inc., 1945.

Wilder, Thornton. *Our Town*. New York: Coward-McGann, Inc., 1938.

Wilkerson, W. R. "Trade Views." Hollywood: *Hollywood Reporter*, August 3, 1938.

Wolfe, Donald H. *The Last Days of Marilyn Monroe*. New York: William Morrow and Company, Inc., 1998.

ABOUT THE AUTHOR

Born impoverished in the Great Depression's worst year, toddler Laura June Williams found care beyond her family. Foster parents showered her with love, but one show business couple embraced her in the lap of luxury in Hollywood's Golden Era. During childhood, she appeared in several episodes of the *Little Rascals* and other films. After attending Berkeley and U.C.L.A., Laura June chose to teach young children in both California and Canada.

In recent years the author wrote extensively for the Kingston (Ontario) *Whig-Standard*, and was a weekly columnist for the Pahrump (Nevada) *Gazette*. She is currently editing the memoirs of two octogenarians, transcribing her own pioneer great-grandmother's 1874-1896 journal, and writing and speaking on end-of-life issues.

Printed in the United States
215787BV00002B/17/A

9 781418 438623